WISEWOMAN'S COOKERY
FOOD, SEX, MAGIC & MERRIMENT

~ A Guide To Aphrodisiac Cooking, Sensual Simples & Folklore Erotica ~

written by shannon loeber & mary elsie edwards

designed by base-10 design & development inc. (base-10.net)
cover design by shannon loeber & mary elsie edwards
photography by shannon loeber & mary elsie edwards
cover photo & colour portraits by bebb studios (bebbstudios.com)
cover model – jennifer edwards
editing consultant – val wilson

The authors have made every effort to contact current copyright holders.
Any errors or omissions will be rectified in future editions or reprints.

Published in Canada by Shannamar Publishing House
Printed in Canada by Friesens

first edition 2009

Mixed Sources
Cert no. SW-COC-001271
© 1996 FSC
FSC

Disclaimer

We, the authors, have tested
our home remedies and recipes
to the best of our ability.
Each person has his or her own
individual tolerance; approach
the recipes with respect.
The author, publisher, editing
consultant and copyright holder
assume no responsibility
for any injuries or damage
caused or sustained while using
the recipes or rituals described
in this book.

dedicated to

This book is dedicated to our families.
We love you very much.

~ In Honour of Mother Earth ~

to our readers

Welcome to an incredible journey into food lore, mystery, and magic.

Our book of cookery is teeming with teachings of wisdom, sexuality, and romance
through food craft, garden alchemy, poetry, healing arts,
love, and nourishment.

We weave passion and a pinch of humour with recipes and folklore erotica,
enabling each reader to discover his or her pleasure senses, participate
in the bounty of nature, and give back a piece of Mother Earth
to lovers, family, and friends.

We grew all the herbs and most of the vegetables in our photographs.
We prepared all the recipes numerous times from scratch, tortured our families
with our early failures, and took pictures of the incredible food and magic
we created in our homes and kitchens.

While working on this book, we visited such venerable institutions as the Lambeth
Palace Library in London, Trinity College, Dublin, and the Folklore Department
at the University College of Dublin. We researched women's lore, folk traditions,
ancient cultures, myths, and other writings and explored the way they relate to the
pleasures of the palate and myriad genres
of food history.

This book is a labour of love.

We hope you enjoy reading it as much as we enjoyed writing it.

For more information, please visit our blog at www.wisewomanscookery.com.

Contents

Food Craft

Aromas in the Kitchen ~ Magical Spells with Magical Smells

The wisewoman's way, practised on an everyday basis, has a positive effect upon us in our daily life, and is especially apparent in the kitchen. Food conjures euphoria by nurturing the body physically as well as altering our chemical and emotional balance. It affects our Health, our Spirituality, and our Sexual Happiness.

Successful conjuring in cooking depends on the will summoned and directed by the cook; this craft is more easily called upon when you have an express purpose, such as romance, nurturing, or healing. With the proper Blessings and the right tools and props, an altered state of mind can be achieved with food and drink.

~ Share Our Journey ~

HERBAL LORE

"The Sun robs the Sea, the Moon robs the Sun,
the Sea robs the Moon and the Earth robs them All."[1]

ℌerbal Lore

To be a good kitchen coquette, you must have a well-stocked kitchen. To us, this means herbs, spices, and the sensual sorcery of real food. Embrace the mystery of each plant and flower and make it part of everyday life in your kitchen and bedroom. Learn how to make old-fashioned simples, erotic washes for erotic places, and great food recipes.

Teaching the woman's lore and usage of each plant, be it for nutrition, healing, or altering the conscious state, was passed from "mother to daughter, aunt to niece, grandmother to granddaughter"[2] for generations. The village wisewoman "offered second sight, healing by touch" and "hope by their blessings,"[3] all through the use of herbs and herbal lore.

As modern wise women we have to learn to take time for ourselves and partake in special moments. This is where the ritual comes in. Make magic potions, herbal elixirs; bless and anoint your body, exalt in your spirit—heal and worship yourself.

Lover's Massage Oil

Lover's Massage Oil

Mint, Eucalyptus, Thyme, Rosemary

Place fresh herbs into a clean bottle and fill with grapeseed oil—let sit for 2 to 3 days, strain and use within 1 week. Use twice as much Mint and Lavender as Rosemary and Thyme.

Spirit Candles

These candles are for those bad juju days. You know those days, when you are zapping light bulbs, bursting glasses, burning dinner; the toilet is plugged and the roof is leaking. Light a Spirit Candle to nourish your environment and harvest happiness in your home. This will kindle the atmosphere with balance and create a calm flow for misdirected energy, tipping the scale from negative to positive.

6 Regular 12" plain white tapers (plain paraffin
or beeswax, with a natural cotton wick)
1 block of canning paraffin
1 natural-bristle artist's paint brush
1 small pot to melt the paraffin
Use a selection of dried or powdered herbs
of your choice: Sage, Oregano, Thyme or Basil

In a pot, melt 1/2 block of paraffin on your stovetop at the lowest heat setting. The cooler the wax, the stickier it is. We use a combination of powdered and dry- leaf herbs, lightly crushed together and added directly to the melting wax. To protect your counter top, cover it with paper. Take the pot off the stove and dip your brush into the wax mixture, painting the herbs onto the candle while the wax is still hot. If the mixture becomes cool, reheat it on the stove.

Rosemary and Sage for protection, clarity, and to clean out heebie jeebies
Mint and Basil for passion, love, and attraction
Thyme for boredom, blues and blocked energy

Before picking or using herbs, offer a blessing and give thanks to the spirit of the plant for its life essence. This will maintain the potency of the herb-magic. Never take the whole plant; allow the old spirit to mix with the new to create new life. Charge the herbs for spiritual protection, fruition and wealth, desire and passion, or a gift of love by using natural crystals or special rocks and shells you have collected. Place them into a bowl with your herbs. When you are ready to release the *Dragon*—the power of the herbs—take the crystals and rocks out of the herbal mixture. Do not leave burning candles unattended.

℘arsley:

The Before and After Sexual Herb

Parsley has long been associated with love and sex in Folklore Erotica. An "Enchanted Parsley Salad," eaten before lovemaking to make all your body parts fresh smelling and kissably exciting, will prime your man for more vigorous sex and make you more amorous and receptive.

When eaten fresh, Parsley can change the taste of a man's sperm, lessening the gag reflex. Soaking in a tub, with a strong brew of Parsley tea and sea salt added, can refresh the *musty-muff* after sex. Drinking the tea can help relieve bladder inflammation caused by *honeymoonitis*, as well. It is healing, nourishing, cleansing, pampering, and refreshing.

Used in infusions to relieve indigestion, bladder and kidney afflictions—for babies' colic and as a wipe for diaper rash—Parsley was found in every woman's still room. A poultice of Parsley can be used to relieve insect bites and stings.

Put a bowl of fresh Parsley on the table for any meal. High in vitamins and minerals, Parsley aids digestion and keeps the breath fresh. Serve in salads, herb butter (for buns and steamed new potatoes), soups, stews, and biscuit dough.

Enchanted Parsley Salad

1 1/2 cup of Parsley flowers
2 med. tomatoes
1/2 small red onion
1/2 English cucumber
1/2 yellow pepper
1 avocado (not ripe, on the hard side)

2 tablespoons grapeseed oil or olive oil
2 tablespoons white or Balsamic vinegar
2 teaspoons lemon juice
2 teaspoons sugar
3/4 teaspoon salt

Cut your salad into small pieces so you can experience a different combination of vegetables with a hint of Parsley in every bite. Pour the oil, vinegar, and lemon juice directly onto the salad. Add the sugar and salt; toss gently and serve.

Parsley Chicken Broth

Adding Parsley to your chicken stock adds a lovely flavour and makes it an even more powerful healer. Bladder afflictions are a common ailment among women. Parsley is still used by herbal healers to help relieve the symptoms.

Soup Stock: Chicken or Turkey

The best soup comes from an organic bird. Most butchers sell backs and necks for a really good price. Throwing in an extra leg or two adds to the flavour. If you want to make a large pot of extra-savoury broth make sure you use enough chicken. Always wash raw poultry.

~ Fully immerse the meat in a pot of boiling water for 3 to 5 minutes. This takes all the fat and sludge out of the bird. Remove and put the meat in a fresh pot of water. Add 1 cup Parsley leaves, 2 to 4 large carrots, 3 to 5 celery sticks, 1 large onion (peeled), and 1 small bulb of garlic (just wash — don't peel).

~ Let this simmer for 3 or 4 hours, add your spices (Sage, Savoury, Oregano, Rosemary, salt, and pepper) and simmer for another 45 minutes. Let cool and put the whole pot and contents into fridge over/night. The next day, skim off the congealed fat and bring it to a boil again. Simmer for half an hour or so, cool, then strain through a colander. If you like a clearer broth, pour it through a strainer. Garnish the broth with fresh, chopped Parsley before serving.

Fresh Breath Dog Biscuit

~ Wet Mixture
    2 jars of organic chicken baby food (100 ml)
    1 1/2 cups of Parsley chicken broth
    3 heaping tablespoons of engevita yeast
    1 teaspoon grapeseed oil
    1 egg (whisked)

~ Dry Mixture
    1/2 cup dried Parsley
    2 cups rice
    1 1/2 cups rice flour
    4 cups rye flour

Mix all the wet ingredients in one bowl and the dry ingredients in another. Add wet to dry and mix until the dough is firm enough to roll out like pie dough. Leave the dough to sit for 7 to 10 minutes. Roll out your dough on a well-floured (rye flour) piece of wax paper. Wet the counter first and the wax paper will stick to the counter. If the dough is sticking to the rolling pin, sprinkle flour on top of the dough, as well. Brush the rolled-out dough with a little organic soy sauce. Cut into biscuits and bake at 375 degrees until crispy (35 to 45 minutes).

Rosemary

Rosemary has always been one of the cherished herbs of the Goddess Foremothers. Infused with spring water, it was used to ground and purify the mind, body, and psyche. Rosemary smudge pots were burned as offerings to keep bad spirits away and were a constant companion in the birthing room, at house blessings, and on the battlefield. They were also used in the sick room to purify the air and prevent infection. Lastly, the Rosemary smudge was burned as a Spiritual offering during burial ceremonies.

Brewed in the kitchen of many a wise woman, Rosemary was used to strengthen the heart, ease congestion, and help tame nervous conditions. A good strong Rosemary/Mint/Chamomile tea with lots of honey will help to gentle the stress of PMS.

The provocative scent of Rosemary awakens the body to sexual arousal in an enchanted way, like a vision or a dream. This beloved herb has long been woven into wreaths and bridal bouquets as a symbol of everlasting love and remembrance. Hung in sprigs above the bed it will help bring harmony into your love life.

Use Rosemary in tomato sauce, soups, and stews or to enhance any meat or fowl.

Rosemary

"Who passeth by the Rosemary
And careth not to take a spraye,
For woman's love no care has he,
Nor shall he though he live for aye."[4]

"where Rosemary flourishes the Lady rules"[5]

Rosemary Smudge

Smudging Rosemary evokes ethereal wisdom; its smoky presence in the air strengthens virtue, stimulates the senses, and improves clarity of mind. To capture a potent blessing, dry branches of a Rosemary plant you have grown yourself. Clip 5 equal-sized pieces about 12 inches long. (The number 5, like the 5 points on the Neopagan pentagram, represents spirit, water, fire, earth, and air. When encased in a circle, the pentagram symbolizes the Goddesss.) Gather the stalk ends of the branches and bind them together with 2 pieces of twine knotted at the end. As you wrap the twine around the stalks, cant or sing a blessing—a wishing of well-being, a charm of protection, the gift of the third eye for inner sight, a bringing of action to manifest wealth and prosperity—each and every time you knot the cord. Wrap the twine one third of the way up the stalk, leaving the end to burn.

Now hang it in a cool dark place to dry for 2 to 3 days.

When you are ready to cant your blessing and smudge either the person you are trying to help or the house you are trying to heal, light a candle and run the fire up and down the Rosemary wand, twirling it at the same time, catching the outer stems on fire. Quickly blow out the flame, allowing the smoke to spirit through the air.

Bestowing the Gift of Clairvoyance

This ritual is for a friend about to set off on a voyage or venture into a new love affair, friendship or business endeavour; to give the ability to forecast unforeseen dangers, and to enhance the gift of premonition. Draw the smoke around the person's aura but do not touch his or her physical body.

"May your feet go on the right path
May you have protection at your back
May you have light about your head to keep you clear sighted
May you have strength and be safeguarded in your travels"[6]

Blessing and Protecting the Home

Smudging a person's home, hearth and safe haven is a Ceremonial Act. Find the lines of power, North, East, South and West and start at the northern most end of the house moving in a circle, covering each point with smoke from the Rosemary.

"May nothing evil cross this door,
And may ill-fortune never pry
About these windows;
May the roar and rains go by.

Strengthened by faith, these rafters will
Withstand the battering of the storm;
This hearth, though all the world go chill,
Will keep us warm.

Peace shall walk softly through these rooms,
Touching your lips with holy wine,
While every casual corner blooms
Into a shrine.

Laughter shall drown the raucous shout;
And though these sheltering walls are thin,
May they be strong to keep hate out
And hold love in."[7]

Rosemary Beef on a Bun

Three basic cuts of meat guarantee a great-tasting roast—sirloin, sirloin tip, or inside round (Baron of Beef). What you are looking for is a nice solid meat with a small amount of marbling for tenderness and gravy drippings. Choose the size according to the number of people you are feeding.

We always rinse any meat before cooking. Slice some garlic—4 cloves for a medium size roast—into slivers and push it into the meat along the fat line of the roast. Do this on both sides. When you slice the meat, you will have garlic in the slice, along the marble of the beef.

Rub the roast with a good covering of olive oil, then a generous amount of coarse salt. Pat on enough mustard to coat the whole roast. Prepared mustard works great. If you want more zest or tang, use Dijon or hot mustard.

For a medium-size roast, take 1/3 cup fresh Rosemary and 1/3 cup fresh peeled garlic and chop together into small pieces. (For a larger roast, use more.) Press this mixture onto the roast, making sure you have a nice thick covering on all sides.

Place the roast on a rack in your roasting pan. You need a rack to get the drippings for your gravy. For darker gravy, add 2 to 3 sun-dried tomatoes to the bottom of the pan. Cut a large onion into thick slices and place around the roast.

Add enough water to cover the bottom of the pan—not much, because you do not want to steam the roast—making sure not to let the bottom dry out during the cooking process. Do not cover with a lid. Bake at 325 degrees for 20 minutes a pound.

Mint: Irresistible to the Tongue

"The only thing worse than a mediocre blow job is no blow job at all."[8]
Conjure up something special in the kitchen to bind your lover with the lingering memory of your mouth—the scent of fresh mint—gives pleasure on the lips, kissing or sharing oral sex . . .

Mint has a well-known sexual history. Hades, god of the Underworld, chose Minthe, a beautiful water nymph, to be the favourite of all his lovers. When Persephone, his young wife, found them locked in fellatio Heaven, she immediately turned Minthe into a lowly plant destined to be trod upon. Although Hades couldn't change her back again, as a tribute to their adventurous lovemaking, he changed her destiny by bestowing a sweet perfume upon her. Thus she would be forever plucked and cherished—the lovely Mint aroma, the thrilling awareness when savoured in the mouth—a constant reminder of the great oral sex they had as lovers.

So call upon the Ancient Erotica of Minthe and create a love-making adventure with the ultimate oral encounter. Make yourself and your partner deliciously edible. Stimulate and intensify the salacious pleasures of love.

Sweet on You Mint-Honey Elixir

~ 1/4 cup fresh Peppermint leaves, compressed and lightly bruised
~ 1/2 cup of liquid honey
~ Take a minute to bless the Mint and give thanks, then empower the herb. Ask for the supreme euphoria of sexual satisfaction.
~ Begin by warming the honey—either in a microwave or double-boiler until the honey is warm—verging on hot, and easy to pour.
~ Remember, you are summoning Sexual Seduction, so take time in choosing the bottle or jar you will be using. Clean and rinse with boiling water. Let air-dry.
~ Place the bruised Mint in the bottom of the clean jar. For a little extra heat, spice it up with 2 fresh chili pepper seeds. Pour the hot honey into the still-hot jar of Mint leaves. Put the lid on and let cool.

Prepare this elixir a few days prior to your intimate encounter, allowing the Mint to infuse into the honey. When the romance starts, heat the elixir and trickle on the penis or clitoris, inviting the lips, tempting the tongue with exotic pleasures and encouraging sensual exploration. It delivers a tingling, cooling sensation and heightens nipple and genital sensitivity. The penis stays erect longer and the clitoris becomes engorged quicker. The Mint numbs the back of your throat, inviting a more pleasurable experience that leaves your breath smelling kissably fresh. Always remember, enthusiasm is essential when giving and receiving oral love.

Another explosive oral delight — alternate mouthfuls of warm mint tea and ice chips
Try humming — the ultimate vibration sensation.

19

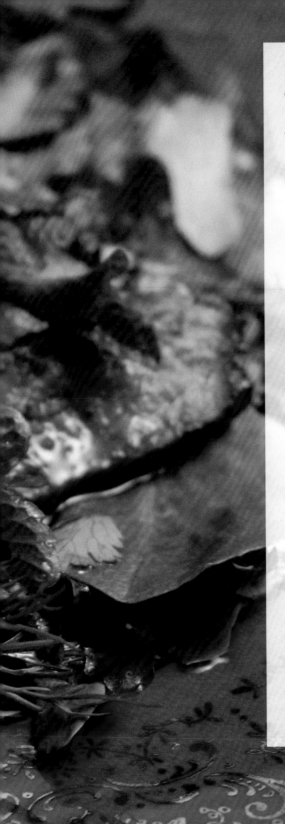

Beef with Mint
on a Bed of Greens

3 medium-sized New York steaks

~ Marinade
  1/2 cup chopped cilantro
  3 cloves of garlic
  3 teaspoons lime juice
  2 teaspoons soy sauce
  2 teaspoons honey
  1 teaspoon hot Asian chili sauce
  1 teaspoon salt

Chop Cilantro and garlic. Add lime juice,
soy sauce, honey, and chili sauce. Rub
the meat with the salt and place in the
marinade. Let marinade for 2 hours.

~ Dressing
  1 clove of garlic
  2 tablespoons lime juice
  2 tablespoons soy sauce
  2 tablespoons rice vinegar
  2 tablespoons honey
  2 tablespoons vegetable oil

~ Combine ingredients in a bowl—let sit.
  1 teaspoon of chopped Mint
  6 cups of mixed greens

Barbeque or broil the steak medium-rare
Let sit for a few minutes, then slice
the meat into strips. Place the greens,
topped with the sliced meat, on a plate.
Crown with chopped Mint and dressing.
Serve immediately.

Bay Leaf

In the ancient Greek city of Delphi, the Bay Leaf or Laurel was consecrated by the sibyls in the temples as a smudge for purifying their mortal self and opening their third eye to herald the truth.

The Oracles of Delphi—a dynasty of Priestesses initiated in the mystic rites of the Oracle—passed down their wisdom through generations, spanning over 1200 years of recorded history (from Homer, 8th century BCE). The priestess would inhale the vaporous breath of the God Apollo, a haze of fumes emitting from the fault in the floor of her inner chamber. It was believed Apollo would enter her body and possess her spiritually, permeating her psyche with the gift of divination. She is shown holding a Bay Leaf, the symbol of the seer and prophetess.

Wreaths of the Bay Leaf were woven and worn by betrothed couples celebrating their nuptial rites as a token of loyalty, truth and everlasting love.

When cooking with the Bay Leaf, keep in mind the magic of this plant. Use as a potent flavouring to any soup, stew, or pasta sauce. Add to marinades for meat, olive oil over goat's cheese or to vegetable cooking water (potatoes, beets, and so on). The Bay Leaf adds an abundance of taste from just one or two leaves.

Brewed into tea, the Bay eaf has a gentle resorative effect for digestive complaints.

Bay Leaf Candle Divination

The Burning Truth

The Power behind "the Truth." Bay Leaf is the Goddess Gift of
Clairvoyance and Divination—become *All Knowing.*

First gather together your divination bowl, rock salt, 2 white bees
wax or lead-free paraffin candles, a metal candle holder,
3 dried whole Bay Leaves, and natural fibre twine or
white cotton string.

Place the rock salt in the bowl around the candle holder. Melt wax
on the leaves from one of the candles and adhere them around the
top of the second candle. Wrap the twine 3 times around the leaves,
securing them in place. Tie 3 knots. With each knot, visualize
the truth you want to unveil.

Secure the candle in the candlestick holder and light it with another
lit another candle. Make sure you watch the candle until the
Bay Leaves and twine have ignited and fully burned. While the Bay
Leaves are burning, incant once, twice, thrice.

3 leaves
3 wraps
3 knots
Power of Nine: Truth Be Mine
Fire of Power: The Full Moon Hour
Truth Unveiled: Deceit Revealed

As the room fills with smoke, You will feel a physical sensation
touching your forehead, thus the opening of your *Third Eye.*

To fully empower Clairvoyance and Communication, this Divination
should be drawn-out on the night of the full moon. For whatever
problem you are trying to reveal, become empowered by the *Truth*
during the night and in the morning the answer will be laid bare,
exposed and brought to light. Depending on the problem, the truth
can take a few days to reveal itself.

Thyme

Thyme has always been known as a favoured Faerie haven, a field of pleasure and erotic play. In Faerie Lore, the real reason people never wanted to leave the land of Faerie is because of the unbelievable sex—being pleasured for days and kept prisoner in your innermost fantasies. It was well known that people caught in a Faerie"s playground were whisked away and entertained with magical food and sex, thus the many tales of the changeling babies, part Faerie and part human. We are always on the look out for a good field of Thyme in which to lay around.

Sexually stimulating, arousing, invigorating, these are the words we would use to describe Thyme. A tea made of this herb increases circulation and promotes a higher oxygen intake, a time-honoured respiratory remedy —both things you want for better, longer-lasting sex. To create a rousing warmth, add a strong brew to your bath. It stimulates the whole body, bringing the blood to the surface of the skin, tingling in the right places— a wonderful way to start a lovemaking session.

Because of its antibacterial and antifungal properties, this same tea can be used as a vaginal rinse for women or a soothing genital rinse for men (great for *jock itch*).

A cauldron of steaming water with a seasoning of Thyme on the stove dispels melancholy and spiritual downtime during sickness. The medicinal steam benefits the lungs and sinus, as well.

Illustration by:
Candyce Raymond

Dried flowers will preserve linens from insect infestation. The dried plant can be crushed and spread around the campsite or kept whole and thrown into the campfire to ward off mosquitoes and black flies. As well, a strong infusion with equal parts of Thyme and Rosemary can be used to heal inflammation from bug and flea bites in both humans and dogs.

Sexually Stimulating Thyme Soak

Whether you just want to make yourself feel sexy or set the mood for a guaranteed romantic encounter, this stimulating salt rub will give you the erotic edge.

This special combination of sea salt and herbs leave the skin tingling and sensitive to the touch, bringing blood to the surface of the skin. (We all know this is a good thing; now you just have to keep it there!) Your senses are heightened by the aroma of the herbs and minerals in the salt as it pulls the impurities out of your body, leaving negativity behind.

Run a hot bath. Have the sea-salt/herb mixture in a bowl beside the tub. Wet your body and stand up in the bathwater. Scoop the bath salt into your hand and rub it in circles in a counter-clockwise motion. This will promote lymph gland drainage, boosting your energy and your immune system. Start with your calves, then rub behind the knee, into the groin area (not on or into the genitals) and over the buttocks and hips; this is also good for reducing cellulite. Let the leftover salt and herbs fall into the bath water. Now sit down in the bath and work on your upper body, massaging the lymphnodes around your chest and under your arms.

Pour the leftover herb salt into the water and immerse your body in the stimulating herbal mixture. This will heighten your senses and encourage the transition from work to play.

Recipe
Mix together . . .
1/2 cup dried Thyme: Stimulating and energizing
1/2 cup dried Sage: Cleansing and purifying
1 cup sea salt: Grounding and protective

"I wish my love was a red red rose growing in a garden fair
And I been the gardener of her I would take care
There is not a month out of the year, but I would see her renew
With flowers fine I'd garnish sweet willow, thyme and rue"[9]

Buns of Desire

These arousing little biscuits are perfect on a date where a romantic interlude is intended. These babies really "spice" up the evening. The herbs we have selected for this recipe not only taste wonderful, they stimulate the body and the senses.

We really worked our *buns* off on this recipe. It was like a science project with the results usually turning out like hockey pucks more than soft, fluffy biscuits.

Here are a few things we learned on our little venture.
~ If you want the biscuits to rise higher, use only white flour and place the biscuits close together on the baking pan. This will brown the top and the bottom, leaving the sides white like a traditional biscuit.
~ If you want a biscuit with a little more fibre, mix half white flour and half whole wheat flour.
~ You can use cold butter or vegetable shortening.
~ For the liquid, you can use cold buttermilk, half yogurt, and half cold milk or soured milk (1 tablespoon vinegar to 1 cup milk).

This is how we make our little biscuits at home.

    2 cups of white flour
    1 teaspoon soda
    2 teaspoons baking powder
    1 teaspoon salt
    1 tablespoon sugar
    3/4 teaspoon Thyme, Rosemary,
    Basil, and Oregano
    1/2 cup cold vegetable shortening
    2/3 cup milk/yogurt

Combine the dry ingredients. Cut the vegetable shortening into the flour mixture, as you would if you were making pastry, to create pea-size clumps of shortening covered in flour. Slowly pour the milk mixture in a circle onto the vegetable shortening and flour, a small amount at a time. Knead together to make a dough. If you handle the dough too much, the biscuits will be hard and heavy. Sprinkle flour on a clean flat surface. Place dough on floured surface and flatten out by hand. Sprinkle flour on the upturned side and roll out with a rolling pin to about 1 1/4 inch thick. Cut out the biscuits and place on a cookie sheet. Bake at 375 degrees for 25 minutes. Serve hot with fresh butter and jam.

Basil: The Goddess Herb Tulsi

In ancient Hindu culture, Tulsi, a type of Basil that flourishes in India, is hallowed as the embodiment of the *Goddess Herself*. Also known as *Holy Basil*, Tulsi is still held sacred to this day, and graces shrines and homes throughout India

Basil creates a clear aura of femininity and loving heart and is a bridge-builder between forgiveness and anger. It effects sympathy between lovers, promising an atmosphere of peace and harmony. Bathing in this blessed herb will cleanse and purify the body and soul in a sacred way. It can brighten your aura and give you a sense of enlightenment.

Mildly sedative when steeped into an infusion and imbibed, Basil tea can make you feel glowing and blissful. It is a divine way to release anxiety and nurse the symptoms of PMS or menopause.

The essence of fresh Basil heightens the erotic pleasure of eating, enlivening the senses with its provocative scent and taste. Invite this herb to the table, experience the feeling of the Goddess.

Add Basil to
Herbal tea (small amount for flavour)
Potato dishes
Pesto and fresh salads
Tomato sauces
Meats and seafood dishes

Sacred Foot Bath:
(Pull negative energy out of the body)
Brew Basil in large pot.
Add sea salt.
Steep mixture.
Do not let cool; this is a hot soak.
Submerge feet and enjoy.

Basil Elixir
Simmer in a pot:
2 cups water
1/2 cup fresh orange juice
1/2 tablespoon Basil and Chamomile
Add honey to taste

Spaghetti with Cherry Tomatoes and Basil

Something about this sauce is truly romantic and sensuous at the same time. The gentle squeezing of the tomatoes with your bare hands, heady with the perfume of the fresh Basi,l manifests feelings of love and euphoria. When eaten fresh, Basil has a mild sedative effect—the perfect setting for Cupid's arrow of love and lust.

1 pound red and yellow cherry tomatoes
2 handfuls of Basil leaves: About 1 cup
6 to 8 tablespoons of extra virgin oil
1 clove of garlic, peeled and finely sliced (more, if you like garlic)
1 tablespoon red or white wine vinegar
Sea salt and freshly ground pepper

1. Cook pasta in a large pot of boiling, salted water until *al dente*.
2. Meanwhile, halve the tomatoes and put them in a large bowl. Add Basil, olive oil, garlic, and vinegar. Season with salt and pepper. Scrunch with your hands to slightly mush the tomatoes.
3. Drain pasta and combine with tomatoes. Taste and adjust seasoning, if necessary. Makes 4 to 6 servings.

Basil

Mint

Isabella; or, The Pot of Basil
A Story from Boccaccio

"She wrapp'd it up; and for its tomb did choose
A garden-pot, wherein she laid it by,
And cover'd it with mould, and o'er it set
Sweet Basil, which her tears kept ever wet.

And she forgot the stars, the moon, and sun,
And she forgot the blue above the trees,
And she forgot the dells where waters run,
And she forgot the chilly autumn breeze;
She had no knowledge when the day was done,
And the new morn she saw not: but in peace
Hung over her sweet Basil evermore,
And moisten'd it with tears unto the core."[10]

Arousing Basil: Love Washing Water

Women who grow Basil in their gardens get more head . . . just ask Isabella . . . (Isabella: from Keats' poem "**Isabella; or, The Pot of Basil**" where Isabella keeps the head of her dead lover in a pot of Basil.)

This little recipe will intensify and prolong the joys of lovemaking, making you deliciously edible with a delicate fragrance and irresistible taste.

Increasing your own sexual allure is not just about getting your hair done; it's about keeping yourself aroused and empassioned. There is something about an aroused woman that really turns on a lover.

To Make This Infusion . . .

If you have the opportunity to grow your own herbs, go out to your garden and gather some fresh Basil and Mint. Always leave some plants to flower, to make your love potions and magical brews even stronger. When the gardening season has come to an end, you can preserve the essence of your hand-picked herbal flowers and leaves by either freezing the selected herbs in ice cube trays or hanging them to dry. (See "Garden Alchemy" page #153.) A number of supermarkets and organic stores sell fresh herbs all year around.

Making an infusion is just like making a strong pot of tea. When using fresh herbs, use a 2 to 1 ratio: 2 cups water to 1 cup herbs. Dried herbal flowers and leaves can be substituted in winter. Use enough to make a potent brew. Infuse for 10 minutes and strain into a bowl. Take a few sips to test the temperature. This wash is best used when it is warm to the touch. After your bath, stand in the tub and sponge the tea infusion onto your genitalia; make sure you lavish your inner parts, as well.

This Elixir of Love will have your nether lips and clitoris throbbing and contracting with the tingling sensation of the Mint mixed with the numbing cool of the Basil flower. You will smell like sweet herbs and clean Mint, while inside pulsing with desire.

Sage: The Spiritual Herb

This age-old herb has been used for generations by Healers and Shamans in almost every culture throughout world. The magic of Sage was a main staple in every Wisewoman's still room and every mother's kitchen. Brewed into a tea or infused in the healing kettle, Sage aids in digestion, stimulates the blood, calms the nerves, restores the memory, and clears the lungs. An infusion of Sage was prescribed for women of all ages, from the reluctant bride, to the young mother during the weaning process (not while breastfeeding), to the matron going through menopause.

Smudging Sage helps attract protection, wisdom, and fruition during rituals and blessings. Fanning the smoke onto oneself opens the door to intuition and foreknowledge. Burning a Sage wand in your home purifies the environment, ridding it of bad ethereal energy. (Be sure to leave the windows open so that the unwanted negativity can escape. When you are finished, clear the smoke and shut the windows.)

Traditionally, Sage has been Eaten on the most sacred of days—Yule-tide/ Christmas, Beltane/Easter, and the Harvest Festival/Thanksgiving. Sage has a good strong flavour and is best used in stuffing for almost any kind of meat, particularly poultry and pork. It is wonderful in soups, stews, herb breads, salad dressings, vegetable dishes, and gravy, to mention just a few.

Sage tea can diminish sexual desire: the very word *sage* means "someone venerated for the possession of wisdom, judgment, and experience".[11] This is part of the charm of old age, when the sex urge has tamed down.

So, if you want to put Pep in your Step or Vex your Sex, Boost your Brain, or Curb the Night Sweats, brew yourself a cup of Sage herbal tea.

Sage

**"He that would live for aye
Must eat sage in May"**

**"Plant your sage and rue together,
The sage will grow in any weather."**[12]

Savory Sage Stuffing

Beyond Festive: Celebration Food

These are some of the words that describe the delicious taste experience this dressing will add to any type of meat, poultry, or fish.

This is a bread stuffing, so the night before, slice 1 1/2 loaves of bread into cubes. We like to use 1/2 whole wheat and 1/2 sour dough. Dry the cubed bread overnight. A great place to do this is on cookie sheets in the oven (turned OFF, with the door closed to keep the pests away).

~Chop 3 to 5 slices of bacon (depending on how much dressing you need). Add equal amounts of sausage meat and chopped giblets and livers, if available.
~Fry in a frypan until a little crispy and drain on newspaper or paper towel.
~In another large frypan, add a tablespoon of grapeseed oil (great for frying) or olive oil and 1/4 cup of butter. Heat the oil and butter hot enough for the vegetables to sizzle when dropped into the pan.
~Finely chop 4 to 6 cloves of garlic, 1/3 cup of each: Onion, celery leaf, and mushrooms. Add to frying pan. Let fry at a high heat, stirring often.
~Add a well-rounded 1/2 teaspoon of each Sage and Savoury and 3/4 teaspoon of each Basil, Oregano, Rosemary and Thyme. If making stuffing for a large bird add 1/4 to 1/2 teaspoon more of each spice.

Put the dry bread cubes into a large bowl. Add the cooked, drained meat and the butter/vegetable/spice mixture to the bowl. This should mix into a fairly moist stuffing. If not, you can do 1 of 2 things. Add more butter to the pan, melt, and add to bread mixture or, if concerned about the butter content, add chicken broth.

Let sit in the bowl and cool off while you prepare the meat for stuffing . . .

Elemental Empowerment with Sage

Sage and Fire: The smouldering fumes of the dried Sage on the fiery charcoal communicates to the spirit world *a sacred smoke*, to carry a divine asking, to permeate the Universe, touching all things.

This is a *Summons of Awakening* for the sleeping winter months, the low energy of winter, when you want to make meaningful changes in your life and need the backbone to do it. Regenerate yourself; clear a pathway toward renewal and clarity; invoke your guardian spirit.

Empowering yourself is a process, but if you do something to visualize your inner strength—keeping it in your mind's eye, recalling it every time you have the need —you will find the fortitude to solve the problem. By smudging the Sage, you are creating an offering so your voice will be heard and you can effect the transformation. Take the time to make a folkway or ritual for 3 nights in a row— before, during, and after the full moon.

In this folkway, we are using the *Power of the Spoken Word* (see page #171) —vocally projecting vibrations to the Universe by chanting and using poetic blessings, to produce magical results. To appeal, invoke, to call upon balance and harmony, here you are using your *words of empowerment*. The most successful asking can be a poem you have written yourself or old poems that call to you from the past.

Light a store-bought coal (a type of incense) or take a burning ember from the fireplace and place it in a fireproof dish. Lay dried Sage leaves on top of the coal, conjuring smoke, your Universal Messenger. Recite your asking, then gently blow on the leaves, turning your body in a circular motion at the same time, completing a spiral, once clockwise, once counterclockwise—North, East, South, and West, whispering acknowledgments to the elements and giving thanks.

North for Earth and Determination
East for Air and Clarity
South for Fire and Empowerment
West for Water and Renewal

SPICE SORCERY

"The herbs were springing in the vale:
Green ginger plants and liquorice pale
And cloves their sweetness offer,
With nutmegs too, to put in ale
No matter whether fresh or stale,
Or else to keep in coffer."[13]

Spice Sorcery

Tales of *the Spice Road, the Spice Islands, the Spice Queen*—China, India, Arabia —exotic memories of times past . . . spice, the word alone conjures visions of erotica and mystery. Utilized since pagan times for worship, prayer, and magic to heighten ritual and ceremony, the arousing aroma of spice awakens the spirit of devotion and inspiration.

The seductresses of every culture—Japanese Geisha. Greek Hetairai, Chinese Concubine, Indian Tawaif, Egyptian Almeh—employed spice as an aphrodisiac to increase performance and potency, burned it as an incense to induce euphoria, and harnessed its mystical powers for magic and healing.

The intoxicating effect of spice can work for you, as it did for Queen Cleopatra when she first met and beguiled Marc Anthony. Known by her enemies as the *Great Whore* (phallus kissing said to be her favourite pastime by all counts of history— 100 Roman nobleman in one night), the renowned fellatrice and heroic queen had to, once again, offer herself to save her people from Roman rule. Using spice and flowers, the bounty of the Egyptian Harvest Goddess Renenutet, she sensually slayed him and gained a brief reprieve for her country. Alas . . . the Enchantress became the enchanted and Cleopatra fell in love. Their legendary love affair tragically ended in death, for both Cleopatra and her love, Marc Anthony.

The "Hymn of Renenutet"

"I will make the Nile swell for you, without their being a year of lack and exhaustion in the whole land, so the plants will flourish, bending under their fruit. The land of Egypt is beginning to stir again, the shores are shining wonderfully, and wealth and well-being dwell with them, as it had been before."[14]

Allegedly, during the reign of Cleopatra VII, the ladies of the evening who took pleasure in the ancient art of fellatio wore the deep red lipstick made from the Carmine beetle.

Or, seducing temptation, spice can work against you, as it did with Pope Joan.

Joan lost everything—her papal crown, her very life—for her love of spicy food. Kings from all over Christendom bowed to her, kissed her ring, asked for her blessing as Pope . . . and she gave up all that . . . for SEX. Knowing what fate awaited her, being stoned to death for being a woman imposter, she still succumbed to the visions of drunkenness and wantonness induced by the power of spicy food and had sex with an intimate college. Of course, fate has it that 9 months later, while trying to mount her horse for a Papal procession, a miracle occurred . . . Pope "John" (Popess Joan) gave birth to a bouncing baby boy.

LA · PAPESSE

The various tales of her ensuing demise include bleeding to death from giving birth at the side of the road, banishment to a convent, hidden by the church for the rest of her days, being dragged through the streets tied to her horse's tail, and stoned to death by the enraged crowd.

It was said that her mother celebrated the Goddess religion. How appropriate that the image of Popess Joan would adorn the High Priestess card in the Tarot de Marseille deck, representing foreknowledge and arcane lore.

Joan allegedly reigned as Pope from 853 to 855 CE.

The scent of spices cooking is an aromatherapy all on its own, tipping the balance toward relaxation and sexual arousal. Symbolic meaning and blessings of intent are bestowed upon individual spices using quartz crystals, semiprecious or precious stones, jewellery, or sea salt, investing the spice with a boon, endowing it with the vibration and specific duties of the crystals. Encircle your glass spice bottles with the appointed crystals and place them on a window ledge to bathe in the full moon. This marries the hidden power of the stone to the spice, which in turn calls upon love, healing, good fortune, or protection to enchant the spice, bringing your charge to fruition.

Invest your own intent into any stone by the use of *the Spoken Word.* Purify your stones to rid them of negativity and other imposing vibrations by covering them in sea salt or soaking them in pure spring water for 3 days.

The Promise of the Stone

Rose Quartz: Heart – love – romance – self-fulfillment – inner peace – forgiveness
Turquoise: Blessed – speaks truth – intuitive gifts – knowledge of folkways
Quartz Crystal: Energy – light bringing – intuition and foreknowledge
Amethyst: Healing – psychic – vibrational connection to the universe
Garnet: Strength of mind – bravery – protection of self – well-being
Jade: Life – health and vigour – protection – companion of luck
Pearl: First love – union – trust – at peace – intuitive power
Opal: Balance – harmony – joy and beauty – dream speak
Sea Salt: Grounding – protection – revokes negativity
Ruby: Sex – passion – success – powerful – focused
Diamond: Strength – happiness – loyalty
Tiger's Eye: Fortitude – determination

Spiced Nuts

Nuts are one of the world's first harvested foods by people on every continent throughout history. Spiced, cooked, and enjoyed in different variations by almost every culture, nuts are an excellent source of protein, a healthy snack, and a tasty addition to any vegetable, rice, or noodle dish.

Five Spice Nuts: This unique mixture of spice represents the five elements in Chinese lore: Water, fire, wood, metal and earth—sweet, bitter, sour, salty and pungent.

~ Preheat oven to 400 degrees. Heat 1 tablespoon of Szechuan peppers in a dry cast iron frying pan for 2 to 3 minutes until you can smell the flavour of the spice.
~ Remove from pan and crush the peppercorns into a bowl with 2 teaspoons Star Anise powder, 1 1/2 teaspoon Fennel powder, 1/2 teaspoon Clove powder and 1 tablespoon Cinnamon powder, mixing all the spices together.
~ Melt ½ teaspoon honey into 1/8 cup soya sauce, let cool. Place 2 cups almonds into the soya sauce-honey mixture. Add spices and thoroughly coat the nuts.
~ Rub a cookie sheet with a light covering of grapeseed oil and spread the coated nuts evenly onto the pan. Bake for 8 to 10 minutes turning them to be sure they do not burn.

The Spell

"Two hazel nuts I threw into the flame,
And to each nut I gave a sweetheart's name.
This, with the loudest bounce me sore amazed,
That, with a flame of brightest colour blazed.
As blazed the nut, so may the passion grow,
For 'twas thy nut that did so brightly glow."[15]

Chili Nuts

~ Mix together 1 teaspoon chopped dried
   chili pepper, 1 tablespoon Cumin,
   1 teaspoon sea salt.
~ Coat nuts with egg-white and add to spice
   mixture. covering the nuts with the spice.
~ Place cashews on a lightly greased pan
   (grape seed oil) and bake for 8 minutes at
   400 degrees.

Cinnamon

If ever there was a spice that betokens love, Cinnamon is it. Burned as an offering for romantic enchantment in Goddess cultures throughout the world, cinnamon has facilitated the art of seduction for many centuries.

When concocted into sweet-smelling oils to anoint and tickle your fancy, or in spicy adult drinks to lure and captivate your lover, Cinnamon has delightful play elements enticing sex and merriment. To experience Cinnamon is to ignite desire.

Sluggish? Can't get turned on? Try eating more Cinnamon.

Applied to the skin, Cinnamon stimulates circulation, bringing the blood to the surface (hard penis, engorged clitoris—hurray!). It also acts as an analgesic, relieving sore, aching muscles. Eating it gives you a feeling of pleasantness and well-being because it helps regulate sugar in the bloodstream (great for diabetics), giving you more energy by not having to deal with the ups and downs of sugar. Cinnamon is an appetite-stimulator, a digestive aid and an aphrodisiac. In many cultures, Cinnamon is still used as one of the main ingredients in remedies for the symptoms of impotence.

Add Cinnamon to
Love potions
Hot drinks: Ciders, toddys, special coffees and teas
Cocoa, honey drinks, almond milk
Fruit punches, sparklers
Honey toast
Fruit salad
Stir frys
Squash
Carrot and sweet potato soups
Baking: Cakes, pies, cookies, sweets and sauces
Bathing: Add to bath sachets

Cinnamon-Dipped Candles

A burning perfume invokes the Goddess for spiritual ceremony and sexual awakening. Its heady scent attracts lust and arouses love companions, conjuring all-knowing visions, revealing the pinnacle of ecstasy and pleasure, the union of two lovers —joining of two souls, the ancient alchemy of the sexual act.

Enhance the musky smell of sex; capture the atmosphere of passion.

Perfume the air with Cinnamon.

Cinnamon and Almond Oil

Cinnamon, the sacred spice of Aphrodite, has been entwined with women and sexuality predating Biblical times. Legend has it that the *Mother Goddess* herself bequeathed the boon of spice to Sheba's first queen, thousands of years ago. As told in the tale of Bilqis, the last Goddess Queen of Sheba, High Priestess to her people: Annointing herself in oil and spice, she lured and captured her infamous lover, King Solomon, connoiseur of women, husband of 100 wives.

Many different tales surround Bilqis's natural body hair, but in the end, King Solomon's fabled *djinns* concocted a cream to expose her legs—we're sure they didn't stop there—thus inventing one of the world's first depilatories. The Queen of Sheba, known to be a seeker of knowledge and wisdom, didn't take long to discover that this not only enhanced her lover's sexual sensations, but hers as well.

Naked flesh . . . an ancient erotic secret of the enchantress for thousands of years when preparing for sexual ritual and body-pleasuring. Be your own *Priestess of Love*—an aroused paramour with ancient feasts, wine, the silk caressing your naked sex with every movement, the vulnerability of being shaven, allowing yourself to succumb to your true love's desire—the exposed woman, the temptress.

Submerge in the heady delight of Almond oil and Cinnamon. Rub them on your shorn nether lips, your breasts. Feel the warming sensation on your clitoris and nipples, the blood surging to the surface of the skin, engorged, feverish for touch.

Cinnamon
Enflames the skin with a rosy flush exciting the senses, a warming exotic feeling, at the same time adding a small layer of protection with its antifungal and antibacterial properties. Cinnamon has its own natural perfume, its sweet earthy scent is enticing and seducing. (The Queen of Sheba's intimate fragrance was a combination of Cinnamon and rose.)

Honey
A gift from the Goddess to Mother Earth, an age-old beauty treatment for skin (Kama Sutra – Cleopatra's beauty secret), antibacterial and invigorating.

Almond Oil
Contained inside the Almond oil is a natural amino acid called L-Arginine. This amino acid is in many of the topical clitoral creams available on the market today. It increases blood flow to the genitals, enabling a woman to acheive a clitoral erection, which is needed to have a clitoral orgasm. Pure Almond oil is easily absorbed into the skin, a perfect carrier for the aphrodisiac essence of exotic spice, great for massage and sexploration—any excess acting as a natural lubricant (use non latex condoms). Our recipe is completely edible, inviting oral sex. Besides, there's a lot to be said for having a pussy that smells like mom's fresh-baked apple pie.

Cinnamon & Almond Oil Recipe

2 cups pure Almond oil – 30 Cinnamon sticks – 1 tablespoon liquid honey
Charge the spice with your desire.

~ Heat the oil. Do not bring to a boil. Stand over it,
  stirring and smelling so it does not burn
~ Place Cinnamon sticks and powdered Cinnamon in
  a heat-proof bowl, cover with drizzled honey.
~ Pour heated oil over the Cinnamon sticks (oil has to be
  hot enough to bubble), gently stir and let cool.
~ Cover and cold infuse in the fridge for 2 weeks.
~ Take the bowl of Cinnamon oil out of the fridge and
  place on countertop, letting oil reach room temperature.
~ Place bowl on a small pot 2/3 full of warm water
  (the bottom of bowl should be immersed into the water)
  and bring the water to a boil creating a *double-boiler*
  effect, gently heating the oil and melting the settled honey.
~ Stir the honey back into the oil, take the bowl off the hot
  water and let the oil cool – strain 3 times through plain
  white cotton or muslin - pour into your chosen bottle,
  cover and store in the fridge – use within 2-3 weeks.

(for a stronger brew, add cassia bark)

*Always test products
for skin sensitivities
on the inside of your
wrist before using
on the most delicate
areas of your body.
If you have nut
allergies, substitute
Grapeseed oil in place
of the Almond Oil.*

Drunken Raisin Rice Pudding

This *hot* pudding (in more ways than one) is meant to be served at an adult gathering, guaranteed to get everyone going . . .

Alcohol and Cinnamon excite and stimulate, bringing on arousing warmth. Top this with whipped cream laced with Grand Marnier and orange zest and Voila! The effect has been achieved . . . the small amount of alcohol in this recipe is just enough to help reduce inhibitions.

Take 2/3 cup of golden raisins (lightly packed) and add Grand Marnier, filling to 1 cup. Soak the raisins in the Grand Marnier for 1 to 2 days! Strain raisins; put remaining alcohol aside.

4 cups cooked Arborio rice
2 eggs (well beaten)
1 cup cream
1 cup milk
1/2 cup brown sugar
2 teaspoons ground Cinnamon
2 tablespoons orange zest
(using the small side, grate the orange skin—no white—of approx. 2 oranges).
1/2 to 3/4 cup sliced Almonds

To bake and serve in individual baking dishes
Mix ingredients (except Almonds) in a large bowl and pour into individual ceramic baking dishes, spooning and pouring out equal amounts of the rice and milk mixture into each dish. Bake at 350 degrees for 1 hour. Liberally sprinkle more Cinnamon and the sliced Almonds on top of the pudding 15 minutes before it is finished baking, allowing the Almonds to roast slightly and the Cinnamon to reach the full measure of flavour.

To bake and serve in one large baking dish
Mix ingredients (except Almonds) in the baking dish and bake uncovered for 1 hour and 20 minutes at 350 degrees. Sprinkle Almonds and Cinnamon on top of the pudding 15 minutes before it is finished baking.

Serve with the ultimate finishing touch: Pour whipping cream over the individual servings, then bombard them with the leftover Grand Marnier. Savour the taste and bask in the *Spirits* of fellowship with this delightful dessert.

Nutmeg

Nutmeg: Aged, venerable, more precious than gold. Exalted in the divine use of magic, in healing, and as an aphrodisiac,

Nutmeg charm bracelets: A gifting of love and protection, a symbol of fidelity, worn to increase clairvoyance

Steeped in wine and spirits, brewed as a love potion, Nutmeg summons a rousing aphrodisiac with pleasant hypnotic effects, leaving lovers spellbound with desire. Isolde, Irish Wisewoman, female Shaman, fell in passionate love with her patient, Tristan. Mistaking the love potion intended for herself and King Mark, her future husband, for the poison that she and her lover Tristan were willing to take to spend Eternity together, they sealed the fates of a kingdom.

Spice up your sex drive and ignite your lover's passion with our *Love Potion*, inspired by the enchanted history of Ireland, infused with the heat and fire of Irish Whiskey and entranced by the euphoria of the nutmeg.

The Art of the Heart Love Potion . . . so Dreamy!

Throughout history, in every culture, it was considered an art and an esoteric skill to be versed in the knowledge and lore of breweress. Recipes for brewing spirits, romantic elixirs, and remedies of the heart were passed down through generations, and the wisewomen who crafted them, were sought after, in the dark of night, by common people and nobility alike

~ Cut a ripe but firm pear in half lengthwise, gently core and cut out the string.

~ Mix together
   1 teaspoon brown sugar
   1/2 teaspoon butter
   1/2 teaspoon Nutmeg
   1/2 teaspoon Cinnamon
~ Stuff mixture into the core of the pear
   halves and place them flat-side-down
   on the bottom of a baking dish.
   Add 1/2 inch of water.
~ Bake at 350 degrees for 40 minutes.
~ When the pears are finished baking,
   place them into a heat-proof bowl.
~ Pour the remaining syrup into a pot.

~ Add
   1 cup of water
   1 teaspoon honey
   2 tablespoon orange zest
   2 large freshly squeezed oranges

~ Bring to a boil; reduce heat and simmer for 3 to 4 minutes. Take off the heat, strain and add 1/2 cup Irish Whiskey and 1 ounce Nutmeg, Poppyseed, and dried pear elixir.

~ Pour over the pears and serve hot with a dusting of Nutmeg.

It is best to buy Nutmeg whole and grate it on to the dish or concoction because previously ground nutmeg is less flavourful and aromatic. To test the Nutmeg, pierce a hole in it. If you see oil coming out, that means it is still fresh.

Nutmeg is a circulatory stimulator, encouraging blood to the genitals. It bolsters sexual stamina, and abates the symptoms of frigidity, impotence, and premature ejaculation. A praiseworthy *Love Spice*.

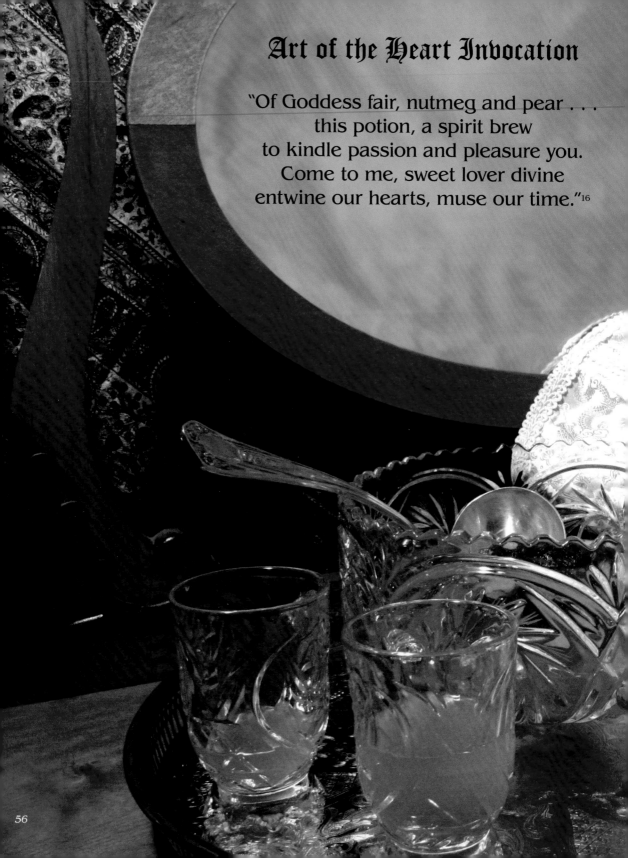

Art of the Heart Invocation

"Of Goddess fair, nutmeg and pear . . .
this potion, a spirit brew
to kindle passion and pleasure you.
Come to me, sweet lover divine
entwine our hearts, muse our time."[16]

Burning Euphoria

This invocation, *Will Wishing*, initiates your intent. Use the power of your will to bring happiness back into focus. Burned during the magic hour—the end of day, the beginning of night—Cinnamon's spicy abundance stimulates the atmosphere, gladdening the living soul, increasing the joy of the *true being*. Nutmeg, the thick spellbinding smoke, alters mood and awakens memory, creating dreamscape, bringing visions and reflections of well-being. Together they summon the protection and strength to enact a shift in conscious thought.

Known to increase mystical powers since the revelation of fire, incense has been used to invoke the gateway to seduction and magic, as a tool for spiritual prayer and religious ceremony and to attract and *will* good fortune, health, love, and protection upon ourselves, our loved ones, and our surroundings. The sacred art of igniting euphoria in a house of worship, on a shrine, or in the boudoir has been celebrated by women from all walks of life since the beginnings of women's cookery.

Cinnamon and Nutmeg, votive offerings appeasing the Mother Goddess, send a vision revealing your pathway. Spice and herbs, first cast upon the fire or brazier—spirals of smoke, channeling invocations and askings skyward to the Universe.

Take time for yourself. Relax, envision yourself surrounded by white light allowing the calm to envelop you. Release the dispiritedness with the burning spice and the rising smoke, meditate, and *Will Wish* inner happiness.

This invocation should be done out of doors. Use a small metal brazier or bowl. Put rocks into the bottom of the bowl. Light your coals (see page #40) and place them on top of the rocks. Break Cinnamon sticks and whole Nutmeg nuts into chunks and add to the burning coals along with a generous amount of ground spice.

Ginger

Taken internally, Ginger fires up the body, relieving the symptoms of colds and flu, aiding digestion (rids nausea), and strengthening the immune system. When stress sets in, a tonic of Ginger increases circulation and restores energy. Mother Nature's only caffeine free stimulant, Ginger has been used as an aphrodisiac and a timeworn restorative for men in every culture that it has visited.

Massage oil infused with exotic and spirited Ginger soothes aches and pains, exciting skin sensations, and lubricating the body for hot sex play.

Herbal tonics and formulas to aid in healing the body and maintain a healthy sexual relationship are listed in ancient texts from India and China dating as far back as 2000 BCE. The *Atharva Veda*—India 2000 BCE—is a magical digest of incantations and formulas, many of which include the spice Ginger.

Add Ginger to:
Vegetable or meat stirfry, baking, tonics or tea.

Serve Ginger:
Dried, pickled, crystallized, or preserved in syrup.

Ginger Bread Love Cakes

Ritual Cakes, offerings to the Goddess, have been celebrated as giftings and fairings since pre-Pagan times, representing the wealth and fruitfulness of the harvest, the gift of plenty.

In the spring, cakes were buried in the fields to appease Mother Nature. In the summer, they were made into the shapes of the sun, moon, or stars, honouring first harvest. Faerie cakes were given as offerings to appease the Guardians of the Forest and honey cakes were placed on graves to quiet the Spirits of the Dead.

The heart-shaped gingerbread cake, the opulent bestowal of love, reveals your intent, saying *I love you*. With each stirring of the batter, bless the cake with love and unwavering purpose.

When the Sun Sinks to Rest

"When the sun sinks to rest,
And the star of the west
Sheds it's soft silver light o'er the sea,
What sweet thoughts arise
As the dim twilight dies -
For then I am thinking of thee!"[17]

Gingerbread Cake

Preheat oven to 350 degrees.

~ Dry Mixture
  2 cups all-purpose flour
  1 teaspoon baking soda
  1/4 teaspoon salt
  1 teaspoon ginger
  1 1/2 teaspoon cinnamon
  1/8 teaspoon clove
  1/4 teaspoon nutmeg

~ Wet Mixture
  1/2 cup butter
  1/2 cup sugar
  2 eggs
  1/2 cup un-sulphered dark molasses
  2 teaspoons orange zest
  1 cup soured milk (see page #176)

Mix dry ingredients.

Blend with an electric mixer (or by hand) the butter and the brown sugar until creamy. Add the eggs, the molasses, and the orange zest, blending as you add each ingredient.

Add flour and soured milk to the wet mixture in three installments, mixing well between each addition. Pour into a buttered cake pan and bake at 350 degrees for 45 minutes.

Glaze

Heat
  1/3 cup orange juice
  1/3 cup honey
  1/2 teaspoon fresh grated ginger
  2 teaspoons orange zest

Simmer for 20 minutes. Let cool. Add 1/3 cup Drambuie. Place in fridge overnight.

Many ritual cakes are still used to this day in every culture in the world. Wedding cakes, birthday cakes, Easter and Christmas cakes are the more familiar ones.

Ginger Ribs

Cut pork baby back ribs into desired lengths so they can lay flat in the pan. Immerse in boiling water for 5 minutes.

~ Marinade
  1/2 cup soy sauce
  3/4 cup liquid honey
  1 flower of garlic
  1 piece fresh Ginger the same
  size as the garlic flower

Peel and grate the Ginger and garlic—add the liquid honey and soy sauce and mix well.

Lay the ribs on the roasting pan and pour the marinade on top. Turn ribs over a number of times, making sure to cover every inch of rib. Lay meat down on the pan in the honey/soy sauce mixture, spooning some on top of the ribs, as well. Put into the fridge overnight. If you have time, turn the meat again the next day.

The ribs take 45 minutes to an hour either on med-low heat in the barbeque (lid down, meat uncovered) or in an oven at 350 degrees (uncovered). Cook meat-side-down and baste a few times during cooking.

Ginger Beef Stir Fry

Vegetables: Ginger (fresh peeled), garlic, onion, celery, red, yellow or orange sweet pepper, asparagus, broccoli stalk (peeled), carrots, cauliflower, mushrooms

Stirfry Sauce: 1/3 cup honey, 1/3 cup soy sauce, 3 cloves grated garlic, 1 piece grated ginger (same size as garlic), 1 tablespoon hoisin sauce and/or black bean sauce, chili peppers to taste.

Melt ingredients together in a small sauce.

Thinly slice all vegetables for stir fry, the portions depending on what you have in the fridge and how many people you wish to feed. Heat grapeseed oil in a large wok to sizzle point, add vegetables (sweet pepper and mushrooms last). Quick fry at a fast heat for 2 to 3 minutes, remove the vegetables from the pan with a perforated spoon to allow the oil to escape back into the pan. Add thin sliced meat to the hot oil and fry on high heat until the meat browns. Add sauce and sprinkle flour or corn starch to thicken. Put the sautéed vegetables back into the pan of meat and sauce, bring to boil, and serve over rice.

Cloves: The Titillating Spice

This intoxicating spice has earned the notoriety of an aphrodisiac (its physical shape resembling the male sex), infusing *sex magic* into any willing participant. Consumed in a drink, stimulating Cloves can be a mood enhancer, delivering gentle earthy arousal, turning on your whole system. Cloves contain eugenol, its gentle numbing effect to the skin, when applied topically, unzips an abundance of sexy good fun.

Cloves promote blood circulation, yielding vital restorative energy, at the same time, easing mental fatigue and anxiety. (Cloves were first documented in historic Chinese writings from as early as 400 BCE.)

Ancient recipes for spicy brews and teas containing Cloves have been recorded as remedies to combat cold and flu symptoms, as an expectorant for lungs, and as a mouth wash for gum disease, cancers, and cold sores. When consumed on a regular basis, Cloves are a time-honoured, all-around tonic, nurturing good health and well-being.

One of the most celebrated tisanes in history is the spicy elixir *hippocras*, a Clove spiced wine named after the famous philosopher/healer Hippocrates, the "Father of Medicine." The seduction of its erotic aroma combined with the therapy of its mind-calming effects and heart-warming afterglow make it a perfect aperitif—a restorative companion of the night.

Recipe for Hippocras

1/2 cup honey
2 whole Nutmegs
4 Cinnamon sticks
1 1/2 whole cardoman
1 1/2 teaspoon sliced dry Ginger (see page # 175)
4 white peppercorns

Heat peppercorns in dry skillet until you smell the essence. Crush spices with a mortar and pestle. Add honey and heat on stovetop. Let cool. Add one 26 ounce bottle of red wine. Cover and let sit for 24 hours. Strain twice with cheesecloth into bottles and let sit in a cool, dark place for 1 week to 1 month.

Clove-Ginger Pleasuring Essence

The Far East is the ancestral home of Cloves and Ginger, two exotic spices cloaked in erotic myth and legend since the beginning of recorded history.

The ancient Chinese handbooks of lovemaking were among the first and most extensive manuals on the mastery of sexual relations. These manuals depict instructions exalting the Iniatress, trained in the mystical arts of the Chinese courtesan—sex, music, poetry, philosophy—an educated, witty companion, in control and desirable.

When mastering the arcana of the Iniatress, one divines lovecraft, the age-old skill of seducing and pleasuring a lover.

Become inspired by the Iniatress in yourself. Bask in the sexual secrets from the past. Enjoy your sensuality, know your lover—this vamps the bliss of intimacy. Feel the sexual empowerment without shame or restraint, experience abandonment and enjoy sex for yourself as a woman, the Goddess.

Take the active role of Sensual Mysticism—phallus stroking—how does he like to be stroked? Men are visual; they like to watch you playing with their penis, exposing and pleasuring yourself at the same time . . . even better. Take off your blouse, wear a sexy bra, bare your breasts. Use your hair (clean and soft) as a sex toy, wrap it around his penis, whip him with it. Wear pearls, remove them and wrap them around the shaft up to the head; enclose them in your hand and gently stroke up and down in a twisting rhythm.

Watch your man masturbate. Learn his self-pleasuring secrets.

Men are a lot quicker to arouse and climax than women. Now enters the skill of prolonging ecstacy—staving off his orgasm. In this scenario, the woman is the facilitator, injecting pleasure into her willing paramour.

One of the earliest Taoist handbooks from the Han dynasty (25 AD to 220 AD), the Teachings of the Dark Girl, tells of the Yellow Emperor (the first Emperor in China) consulting the Dark Girl (a mythical guide to the arcana of sexuality and lovemaking) in pursuit of life everlasting, attained through the pleasures of sexual intercourse. Through a series of conversations, and a different approach to the breath of life, she teaches him to retain his yang essence by prolonging his orgasm, at the same time reaping the ecstasy of yin essence from as many women as possible. The end result being an explosive orgasm when he finally does come.

If you want your man to get the most out of his climax, use this recipe and try this technique . . .

Clove-Ginger Pleasuring Essence Recipe

This warming and numbing essence prolongs the joy of lovemaking. The Ginger improves the circulation on the surface of the penis and the Cloves provide a numbing effect enhancing the erection; your lover's passion is increased.

Ingredients: 1/3 cup Almond oil, 1/4 cup cloves, 2 tablespoons dried Ginger slices (broken not powdered), 2 tablespoons of scented coconut butter, 1/4 teaspoon pure beeswax

Put the Cloves and dried Ginger slices into a heat-proof bowl with the oil. Place the bowl over a simmering pot of water, creating a double-boiler effect and infuse the oil with the Cloves and Ginger for about 20 minutes. Take off heat, let cool, and place in the fridge, allowing the decoction to cold-infuse for 48 hours. Reheat, using the double-boiler method, strain through cheesecloth, and put aside. Now melt together the coconut butter and beeswax in a separate pot (stainless steel, glass, or enamel), add the strained oil, and whip together with a hand-held frother or whisk. Add 1 to 2 drops of vitamin A to help preserve the cream and give it a golden hue.

The Technique

"The closer he gets to the summit of orgasm, the more withdrawn his testicles become. His scrotum will usually shrink, unless it is really hot out. Firmly wrap several fingers around the top of his scrotum (at the base of his penis) and grasp his balls in your hand. Get them as fully distended and stretched away from his body as is comfortable for him. The trick is to pull and stretch them, but not squeeze or crush them with your grip . . . think of your fingers acting as a "collar" around the top of his scrotum. As you get to know and love his balls, you will find they can stretch, the more you work them. Firm tugging will actually stop a too-fast orgasm.

If you can time the scrotum—tugs with one hand, while stroking his penis with your other hand, and synchronize the up and down strokes—he will not only be amazed at your skill, but will allow you to play at will with his prized possessions ANYTIME. Later, he will be more relaxed, not in a hurry, and ready to please you at length."[18]

As this is a *melting cream* and is more exhilarating when applied cold, it is best stored in the fridge.

Peach-Clove Flower Cake

Strain the juice from 2 cans of sliced peaches. Cover the strained peaches in Brandy. Add 20 to 25 whole Cloves, soak overnight. Strain and set leftover syrup aside. Preheat oven to 375 degrees.

Sift Together:

2 1/4 cup cake and pastry flour
1 teaspoon baking powder
1 teaspoon soda
3/4 teaspoon salt

Prepare:

1 cup soured milk. Add 1 table-spoon of vinegar to 1 cup milk

Cream Together:

3/4 cup sugar
1/2 cup soft butter
3 teaspoons leftover Brandy syrup

Add 3 unbeaten eggwhites to creamed butter and sugar. Beat at high speed with electric mixer until stiff and fluffy. Add the flour and milk alternately in thirds. Stir by hand starting and ending with the flour.

Grease two 8-inch round cake pans. Line the bottoms with parchment paper. Pour 1 1/2 tablespoons melted butter on top of the paper in each pan. Spread 1/2 cup brown sugar evenly over the melted butter.

Place 1/4 moon peach slices and Cloves on top of sugar arranging like the petals of a flower. Add cake batter 1/2 portion to each pan.

Bake at 375 degrees for 24 to 26 minutes until the cake pulls away at the edge of the pan. Insert a toothpick into the middle of the cake. If it comes out clean, the cake is done.

Remove from pan after cake has cooled for 4 to 5 minutes, otherwise the cake can stick. Run a butter knife around the inside of the pan, turn upside down on a plate and gently shake the pan from the cake. Serve with a generous helping of the Brandy-Peach syrup.

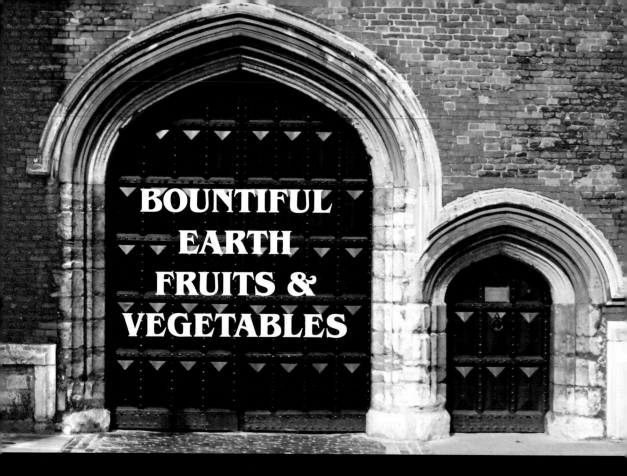

BOUNTIFUL EARTH FRUITS & VEGETABLES

"Were you the earth, dear Love, and I the skies,
My love should shine on you like to the sun,
And look upon you with ten thousand eyes
'Till heaven waxed blind, and 'till the world were done
Whereso'er I am, below, or else above you,
Whereso'er you are, my heart shall truely love you."[19]

Bountiful Earth Fruits & Vegetables

Bountiful Earth, Universal Mother, Heart of the Earth, the Mother Goddess—Creatrix of all forms of life, reigning over all. Representing women, the body of the Goddess—the Earth, a symbol of all fertility: From the sacred gift of the Goddess comes the bounty of the harvest. In the "hunter-gatherer" society, spirituality awakened from the mysteries of Mother Earth, everywhere we look, we see Her (the mother), Her Earth-bound spiritual presence encompasses us, affecting all forces of nature.

First we worshipped the Earth Mother, for all life came from Her. The cycle of life, death, and rebirth, unfolding through the changing seasons were seen as manifestations of the Mother Goddess, Earth, for out of death comes life, and from this, She bestowed the gift of hope upon her people. To appease Her through feasts, offerings, fertility rites and sacred sex, to ask for the miracle of the rain, the rebirth of the sun, the fruitfulness of the Earth, we paid homage and celebrated Her—Mother Nature.

Myriad ancient civilizations call upon the mysteries of the Mother Goddess, revealed by many different statuettes and shrines found throughout history.

Gaia: Greek Earth Goddess: The earth was believed to be her actual body. She gave birth to the Gods.
Isis: Ancient Egyptian Goddess, giver of life and the divine wisdom of womanhood. She assumed human form to teach her people how to cultivate the Earth.
Inana: Sumerian Goddess, all-powerful Mother, predating the Babylonian Goddess Ishtar and Greek Goddess Demeter in the worship of the cycle of nature, death, and rebirth.
Yemaya: West African Mother of all waters, birth-mother of all life.
Pachamama: Incan Earth Mother Goddess of nature and fertility, centred in the earth; her dark side: earthquakes.

Sex and the Goddess Queen

The High Priestess and Goddess Queen would adorn the mantle of the Goddess Incarnate for feasts and celebrations, investing the mystical power of sex for worship: The divine energy, a potent spiritually charged ritual to appease the Great Mother—their womanhood, a symbolic blessing of pleasure—the mystical vessel.

The gifting of food was the offering: Feasts to celebrate birth and life, the harvest, the coming of age, Solstice (mid-summer and mid-winter) and Equinox (spring and autumn), the celebration of the moon cycle, planting, the hunt, war, marriage, puberty, fertility, housewarming, baby-naming, and as a symbol of life passing, given as a final doorway to the otherworld.

Feel the power of the Goddess, glorify life, have feasts. Drink in the divine essence, the pinnacle of sexual excitation with your lover—ecstatic delight, the pathway of the mysteries. Eat and imbibe to entice a desired state. Induce love, ignite desire.

"When the Sultan Shah-Zaman
Goes to the city Ispahan,
Even before he gets so far
As the place where the clustered palm-trees are,
At the last of the thirty palace-gates,
The flower of the harem, Rose-in-Bloom,
Orders a feast in his favorite room–
Glittering squares of colored ice,
Sweetened with syrop, tinctured with spice,
Creams, and cordials, and sugared dates,
Syrian apples, Othmanee quinces,
Limes, and citrons, and apricots,
And wines that are known to Eastern princes;
And Nubian slaves, with smoking pots
Of spicëd meats and costliest fish
And all that the curious palate could wish,
Pass in and out of the cedarn doors;
Scattered over mosaic floors
Are anemones, myrtles, and violets,
And a musical fountain throws its jets
Of a hundred colors into the air.
The dusk Sultana loosens her hair,
And stains with the henna-plant the tips
Of her pointed nails, and bites her lips
Till they bloom again; but, alas, that rose
Not for the Sultan buds and blows,
Not for the Sultan Shah-Zaman
When he goes to the city Ispahan.

Then at a wave of her sunny hand
The dancing-girls of Samarcand
Glide in like shapes from fairy-land,
Making a sudden mist in air
Of fleecy veils and floating hair
And white arms lifted. Orient blood
Runs in their veins, shines in their eyes.
And there, in this Eastern Paradise,
Filled with the breath of sandal-wood,
And Khoten musk, and aloes and myrrh,
Sits Rose-in-Bloom on a silk divan,
Sipping the wines of Astrakhan;
And her Arab lover sits with her.
That's when the Sultan Shah-Zaman
Goes to the city Ispahan.

Now, when I see an extra light,
Flaming, flickering on the night
From my neighbor's casement opposite,
I know as well as I know to pray,
I know as well as a tongue can say,
That the innocent Sultan Shah-Zaman
Has gone to the city Ispahan."[20]

The Earth Bake

All feasts were blessed with *Earth Bakes*, the first baked food was either wrapped in leaves or encased in clay and placed in a banked fire pit on a bed of hot ashes to slow-cook throughout the day. We like baking this dish with sweet garden vegetables simmering in a sauce touched with Ginger, herbs, and maple syrup.

Ingredients: 1/4 cup olive oil, 1/4 cup Balsamic vinegar, 2 tablespoons soy sauce, 2 tablespoons maple syrup, 2 tablespoons barbeque sauce, 1 tablespoon grated fresh Ginger, 1/2 teaspoon of each Rosemary, Basil, Oregano, and Thyme.

Mix ingredients, leave sit while you prepare your vegetables, to allow the herbs to bloom. Add the vegetables to the sauce and place in the fridge, tossing them every so often to allow the marinade to soak in. Use vegetables that won't fall apart in the slow-cooking process: Carrots, beets, potatoes, sweet potato, parsnip, onion, and garlic. We add cauliflower and peeled broccoli stalks. For this dish we used a water-soaked clay pot, but any baking dish with a lid will do (slow-cookers work, as well). Bake for 4 hours at 275 degrees. If possible, baste 2 to 3 times during the cooking process.

Country Cobbler

3 medium apples
2 ripe pears
2 ripe peaches
1/3 cup all purpose flour
1 cup quick oats
(cooks in 3 to 5 minutes)
1/3 cup brown sugar
(lightly packed)
1/3 cup soft butter
1 teaspoon of cinnamon
1/2 teaspoon of nutmeg
1/4 teaspoon clove
1/2 teaspoon salt

Peel and core the fruit and slice it into a well-greased baking dish (canned fruit is optional—strain first). Combine the dry ingredients. Pour melted butter on top of the dry ingredients and lightly mix together with a wooden spoon. Put this mixture on top of the fruit in the baking dish to create a crust. Bake at 375 degrees for 40 minutes.

Tomato:
La Pomme d'Amour
Love Food

The juice of La Pomme d'Amour is and has been a main ingredient in the preparation of love-inspired sauces and stews for generations, whether it be for family comfort and gatherings or sexual sustenance for two. The tomato contains the largest quantity of lycopene of any fruit or vegetable, a powerful anti-oxidant with the ability to lower hypertension and blood pressure. It is also an important food for prostate health, proven to increase fertility and virility.

A *nightshade* plant, the tomato was at one time, suspected of being poisonous like its relative's henbane and belladonna. This connection to poison cloaked the tomato in mystery and, as always, mystery revolves around sex and allure. How ironic—one of the most famous poisoners in *herstory*, a noted herbalist and practitioner of sorcery and astrology, Caterina (Catherine) de Medici (1519 – 1589), daughter of the Italian Duke of Urbino, Queen of France (wife of King Henry II), was the first to introduce the art of the sauce to the French courts.

A sauce made from garden-fresh tomatoes—the stimulus of the herbs added, its anti-oxidant properties and high vitamin C content—will rouse any unsuspecting lover. The blood-rich colour and exotic taste add aphrodisiac qualities to any meal.

Love-Apple Seduction Food

This savouring sauce ignites the passion. The carbohydrates in the noodles deliver a slow-burning energy, enabling you to frolic throughout the night. In the time it takes to cook the pasta, awaken the atmosphere, put on a delectable dress and throw away your panties, the sauce has simmered to completion.

This dish is special because the wine is added to the sauce upon serving. A small port or sherry glass filled with wine accompanies the plate to the table. Pour a small amount (to taste) on top of the sauce and pasta; the wine delivers an adult infusion of full-bodied taste.

Ingredients: 1 medium onion, 4 large cloves of garlic, fresh celery leaves from the inside of the celery or 2 stalks, 2 to 3 medium carrots, 1 large can of whole, stewed tomatoes or 6 to 8 freshly grated tomatoes (see page #175), 1/4 cup Olive oil, 2 tablespoons butter, 1 tablespoon of each Rosemary and Basil, salt and pepper to taste. Full bodied dry red wine.

Cover the bottom of a medium sized-pot with olive oil, about 1/4 inch deep. Add 2 tablespoons of butter and heat until the butter melts into the oil. Now sauté your garlic, onion, celery, and carrot until they soften. At this point, add your stewed tomatoes and spices. Simmer for 30 to 45 minutes. If the sauce cooks down too thick, just add a touch of water. The wine is not cooked in the sauce. Weave the love and bless your food.

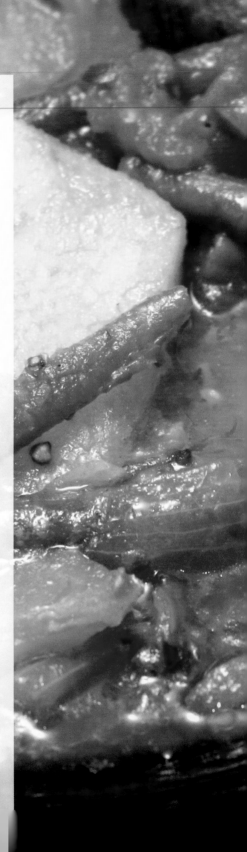

Mediterranean Stew

1 medium onion
5 to 7 cloves of garlic
30 green beans (more if you like)
4 medium-large potato
2 medium zucchini
5 to 6 carrots
Olive oil
Tomatoes

~ Cut the onion into large pieces. Clean and peel the garlic.
~ Pour 1/2 cup of olive oil into a large pot. Heat the oil to a sizzling point. Oil should be hot enough to sizzle when you add the vegetables; this keeps them fresh and crispy. Add onions and garlic. Cook for 3 to 4 minutes at medium-high heat. (Keep vegetables sizzling).
~ Clean and cut beans into 3 inch pieces. Add to pot and sauté 3 to 4 minutes. Peel the potatoes and wash the carrots. Cut into large chunks and add to the pot. Sauté for 5 to 6 more minutes. Cut zucchini into 1 inch pieces, add these last. Continue cooking at a brisk pace until the vegetables are lightly browned on all sides.
~ Preheat oven to 350 degrees.
~ Gently stir in 1/2 can of stewed tomatoes or 6 to 8 large, ripe, tomatoes—grated. (to grate fresh tomatoes see page #175).
~ Add 2 teaspoons each of Basil and Oregano and 1 teaspoon of Rosemary. Salt and pepper to taste.
~ Pour your Mediterranean Stew into a baking dish. Bake at 350 degrees for 45 minutes until the potatoes and carrots are sufficiently stewed.

Garden Beetroot

Some of the first recorded recipes for the beetroot came from a Roman cookbook derived from a collection of recipes originating in the kitchens of the notorious food connoisseur Marcus Gavius Apicius (the Anthony Bourdain of his time), called *The Art of Cooking*. Even in those erstwhile times, the beetroot was recognized for its curative abilities and nutrient-rich value.

Deservingly acclaimed for its aphrodisiac properties for thousands of years, the beetroot contains a mineral called boron, which boosts sexual function; an amino acid, betaine, which combats depression; and natural fruit sugar that easily converts to energy in the body (the beetroot has the highest sugar content of any of the vegetables).

Cut a beet in half, it will reveal the cycle of its life cradled in the earth, a circle within a circle within a circle—the never-ending wheel of life, spirals connecting circles—sex magic, the blood red-colour of the beet creating a visual energy. The *painted body*, an offering for sex, ravishment, the ritual of painting the virgin . . . the ritual to become King—Hieros Gamos—the Sacred Marriage.

The tale of King Arthur and his half-sister, Morgaine (Morgan le Fay), painted with magical signs; the Virgin Huntress to his King Stag. As the offering from the Goddess to her people, the virgin priestess was given in the ritual of the Sacred Marriage to the would-be king, the boy, just come to manhood, Arthur. Both emblazoned with mystical icons, the King Stag joined as one with the Avatar of the Goddess, Morgaine. The graphic symbols adorning their bodies enlighten sexual spirituality where man and woman are consecrated to **God and Goddess**.

Sacred Ink

Body painting is an offering, a primal art, practised for centuries throughout most of the Eastern cultures (India, Turkey, Persia), the African countries, Pagans (Celts), the First Peoples of the Americas, the Aboriginal Australians. It is a pathway to the divine—mystical symbols on the chakras, to open the body to the life wave of the planet, vision and awareness, empowering and protecting.

Bodily adornment for offerings, bridal rituals, rites of passage, mating ceremonies, and preparation for warfare—painted with magical signs for spiritual protection and physical prowess—a magical trance, the hypnotic effect of colour on the skin, the universal language of earthly delights—head, breast, belly and sex.

Call upon the oracle of the sex-moist earth, experience the power of preparation, the anticipation of what's to come, the edge of sexual adventure. The pigment found in beets, is a high-resonating colour, a visual ambiance of reds and oranges to arouse the longing for the enchantress.

~ Anoint your breasts—decorate your body for sexual offering.
~ Paint your lover with ancient symbols of sex and abandonment—the luring, the enticement, the willingness to surrender to the symbols and your lover.
~ Paint the hands—savour the look of the hands on the naked body, caressing, holding (the swollen sex of your desire)
~ The painted feet—the intoxication of pleasure—sucking on toes.
~ The feel of the brush - the anticipation of the "painted one".

Sacred Ink Craft

Hailing from cultures of antiquity, the alchemy of sacred ink is born, transforming symbols and images into living magic. Awaken the mythical power stored in the ink. Charge the intent and manifestation of your desire, embody the paintings of empowerment expressed through your sexuality and love. Sacred ink, a seduction ritual—visible to the naked eye to intensify the sexual act.

Clean and cut 5 beets (leave the skin on). Use a juicer to juice the beets and make 1 cup of beet juice. Strain the beet juice through a fine cheese cloth. Pour the beet juice in to a pot - add 1/3 cup of white vinegar. Simmer for 5 minutes. Add dye thickener (3/4 teaspoon Sodium Alginate).

Simmer for 10 more minutes constantly stirring the thickner into the juice. Let cool to allow the ink to set. If you do not have a juicer - fine grated and strained beets will work just as well with a few more beets to make up a cup for juice.

Mother Earth Spinach Salad

This quick and easy salad is iron-rich, great for those days when you're feeling tired and need a bit of a pick-me-up.

Ingredients:

Beets: Raw, peeled and grated,
steamed or boiled, peeled, chilled
sweet pickled, sliced or diced
Freshly washed spinach leaves
Sweet onion, sliced thin
Orange sections, fresh or canned
Sliced Almonds, optional
Feta cheese, optional

Mix the spinach, beets, sweet onion and orange sections in a bowl. Sprinkle with feta cheese and sliced almonds.

Dressing: Mix fresh orange juice and real mayonnaise to taste. The amount of each ingredient can vary depending on individual preference and number of people.

The beet is an excellent restorative, a blood builder and purifier, a valuable iron source for women. The nutrients promote calcium health and the natural fibre acts as an intestinal cleanser.

Serve beets freshly grated in salads, steamed, in soups and stews, pickled or juiced.

The beetroot is perfect for open-fire baking and the leaves of the beet when steamed are similar to spinach and swiss chard. They are best served topped with butter, a pinch of salt, and a hint of fresh lemon juice.

How to peel a beet. Cut off the beet greens (leave approximately 1 inch), boil or steam until they are soft, run under cold water and rub off the skin.

How to make the broth: We like to use beef marrow bones and beef brisket to make a beef broth, but you can use chicken broth (see page #10) if you prefer.

Borscht
Fill a large pot 2/3 full of water.

Add:
2 large beef marrow bones
2 pieces beef brisket
10 to 12 peppercorns
2 Bay Leaves
1 tablespoon Thyme
1 tablespoon salt
1 large onion
4 pieces celery
3 large carrots
1 whole garlic bulb
Simmer 4 to 5 hours
Let cool overnight
Skim the fat off the top.
Simmer another 2 hours.
Strain and separate meat.

Add:
3 large grated beets
4 quartered medium potatoes
1 large chopped onion
4 large carrots, cut into large pieces
2 small cloves of garlic, diced
2 cups chopped cabbage
Simmer until vegetables are tender.
Add cooked beef from brisket.

To serve: Add one teaspoon apple cider vinegar and a large dollop of sour cream.

The All-Seeing Potato

In the darkest root cellar, during the cold of winter, there lays the potato, sprouting new growth. Revered as life-giving by many civilizations, referred to as *mother seed* by the Incas (the potato was the main food staple that enabled the Inca civilization to exist), the potato has a Goddess Spirit representing fertility and change.

Women in North, Central, and South America were the first to unearth and cultivate this wholesome gift from the soil. Once thought of as poisonous (a member of the nightshade family) and later used solely for animal fodder, the potato became the bearer of life to many desperate people, nutritious enough to keep a family alive throughout the lifeless cold winter months.

Mary's 83-year-old mother told us her memory of the potatoe during the depression, life on the Canadian prairies was challenging; food was scant. Her eldest sister, who at that time was 11 years old, would walk 1 mile each way in the freezing snow to deliver lunch to her brothers at school—a hot baked potatoe, their only food—keeping her hands toasty on the way and still hot enough when they met to fill their stomach with something warm and nourishing.

Not only a food, the potato was used as a folk remedy by many early settlers. Its ability to hold the heat led to the potato being used as a poultice for congested chests and sore throats. Grated fresh and applied directly to burns, inflammation of the skin (eczema), swollen joints (sprains or arthritis) and puffy eyes, the active enzymes released during the grating process can reduce the swelling and draw out excess fluid.

"I'm a careless potato, and care not a pin
how into existence I came;
If they planted me drill-wise, or dibbled me in,
to me 'tis exactly the same.
The bean and the pea may more loftily tower,
but I care not a button for them;
Defiance I nod with my beautiful flower
when the earth is hoed up to my stem."[21]

The Five Secrets of the Perfect French Fry

The first secret is to use vegetable lard, not oil (we like Crisco, used by Shannon's father in his restaurants for years). It is important to preheat the lard, not burn it.

Wash your potatoes, peel them if you want. (Mary likes the skin on, she says it is for nutrition but I think she's just lazy, lazy, lazy.)

The second secret to a crispy fry is in the cut. The thinner the crispier.

The third secret is to put your thin-cut fries into a large bowl and run cold water over the fries until the water is clear and all the potato starch is rinsed off.

The fourth secret is to add a small amount of sugar to the water so the potatoes will turn a nice brown (about 1 teaspoon to a large bowl of fries). Let them sit in the fridge for ½ hour or so.

The fifth secret is placing the potatoes into the preheated lard. Keep a thin layer of water around the fry when you throw it into the pot; that keeps the fat out of the potatoe allowing the potato, allowing the potato to become crispy.

Drinking raw potato juice (including the skin) expels toxins in the body and is an age-old remedy for rheumatism and many other health problems. Make sure you select an older potato (not green), wash well and cut out any eye sprouts and bruise spots. To make a nicer tasting juice, add celery, tomato, and a small amount of onion and garlic. Salt and pepper to taste.

The Potato Ritual

The Spiritual Healer would teach the art of summoning sympathetic magic to their patrons to enable them to visualize their intent and manifest healing. They were a recognized guide to the Other World, affecting health, happiness and spirituality, prescribing life practices to enforce change.

Employ the power of attraction. Enter upon this Ritual for transformation and awareness. The potato represents cultivating a new future hailing from the past. Use the life-stages of the potato to represent the many aspects of being that one hmust go through to achieve a goal—intuition and awareness are symbolized by its all-seeing eyes.

~ Choose your potato—one with many eyes. Give thanks and envision your path. With that in your mind's eye, place it in a paper bag somewhere cool and dry, allowing the new life to germinate. In the darkness of the beginning—sprouting your dream, your desire, your life affirmation. (To guarantee the sprouting process, buy a seed potato at your local garden shop.)

~ Planting—the Future: Ask the Incan potato Goddess Axo-mama for the affirmation of your problem solved. Once again, use the *Power of the Spoken Word* (see page #171). If you do not have a garden, choose a large, deep container. Fill the container half-way full of dirt and plant the sprouted potato approximately 8 inches down if you do not have a garden—always plant below-ground crops when the moon is waning, going from full moon to no moon.

~ With first shoots of green—the realization that your dream is awakening; you are working toward your goal and seeing progress.

~ As you continually bank the dirt you are feeding the metamorphosis of your life (to grow potatoes, you must pile dirt in a mound around the plant as it grows, leaving only the top leaves sticking out—this is called banking the dirt and must be done at least twice during the lifespan of the plant). You have confirmed your intent, now you need to work hard at visualizing what you want, set realistic objectives where you can see your progress with the growth of the plant, allow the attraction, believe in yourself.

~ Harvesting: When your potato plant flowers you are close to achieving your objective. Bask in the beauty of the flower and know that what you have asked for is attainable. When the flower is gone and the plant dries up and turns yellow, your potatoes are ready to harvest. This symbolizes the death of one thing and the life of another.

~ Now that you have harvested your potato, cook and eat it. Celebrate and offer thanks and gratitude, knowing that with every bite, you have reached your goal, "I've reaped the gifts of the Universe; here I am eating my potato."

When *Asking* the Universe to enable change—in your personal life or work-place, with friends or family, allow enough time for the shift to transpire.

"But potatoes now, are a different thing,
They want to grow down, that is plain,
But don't ye see, you must plant for that,
When the moon is on the wane!"[22]

The Amorous Pizza

Garlic and onion, both known stimulants, combined with potatoes, create a food marriage made in heaven—an adult pizza, a perfect side dish for an amorous repast. ("they (potatoes) increase Seed and provoke Lust, causing Fruitfulness in both sexes"[23])

Add 1 clove of chopped garlic and 1/2 teaspoon of Oregano into 3 tablespoons of olive oil. Let marinate while you prepare the rest of the pizza.

For a quick and easy solution to the pizza crust, we buy premade frozen bread dough; we find it's quick and affordable and has that homemade taste that makes this pizza special. Let the bread thaw out on a plate. One loaf makes one 12 inch pizza. Sprinkle flour onto a clean, dry counter. Roll the bread dough onto the flour, completely covering it. Place the dough into an ungreased baking pan (either a pizza pan or a cookie sheet). Knead (punch, to get the air out) and stretch the dough into a flat pizza crust.

Now paint the crust with a thin coat of the marinated oil. Cover with 2 cups of thinly sliced mozzarella cheese. Add sweet onion, garlic, potato, sweet potato, salt and black pepper. Bake at 400 degrees until the crust is golden brown.

Potato Soup

Ingredients:
2 to 3 medium-to-large white or yellow potatoes
3 celery sticks, the inside ones with the leaf
1 large leek
1 clove garlic
2 to 3 carrots
1 small can of sweet corn niblets
1 teaspoon of Basil
1 teaspoon of Oregano
Salt and pepper to taste
Milk to cover the vegetables with milk
1/2 cup water, vegetable or chicken broth

Chop everything quite small, especially the leeks and garlic.
Cut the carrots down the middle at the thick end first. Slice into thin pieces
Cut the potatoes into quarters length wise and then slice as thinly as the carrots.
Leave the starch on the potatoes; it helps thicken the broth.
Allow the milk to warm up to room temperature by taking it out of the fridge 1/2 hour before you need it.
Put a small amount of light vegetable oil into a saucepan. We like grape seed oil. Add 2 tablespoons of butter and heat the oil enough so that the chopped vegetables sizzle when you add them to the pan.
Add the leeks and garlic first, then the celery and carrots. Now add the potatoes.
Let this simmer until the potatoes and carrots are just beginning to soften; then add the milk and either water, vegetable or chicken broth.
Add the Basil, Oregano salt and pepper.
Do not to let this soup come to a full boil.

The Carrot

Roots and berries were the primary foods of early humanity, thus the discovery of the wild carrot. Grown by the ancient Babylonians as an aromatic herb and later recorded by the Greeks and Romans as a medicinal remedy, the carrot was believed to be a cure for a long list of maladies—night blindness, healing from food poisoning, memory loss, and of course, sexual dysfunction.

Carrots were prescribed to arouse and excite sexual desire. This was effective because of the way people ate—meat and very few vegetables. The carrot contains the most carotene—a key anti-oxident—of any other vegetable. The body converts carotene into vitamin A, one of the most important vitamins. The carrots combination of a high amount of natural sugar and its remineralizing and blood-cleansing properties, give the effect of well-being and revitalization.

The phallic shape of the carrot has made it a bedfellow for sexual stimulation and masturbation since ancient times. Women who were trained in the arcane knowledge of love—sexual companions—all used the art of masturbation and the manipulation of dildos to explore their intimate self—not only to discover their erogenous zones of pleasure for greater personal satisfaction, but to strengthen and tone the pubococcygeus muscle to milk the penis during ejaculation.

Self-touch while making love equals contented partners. A woman who can reach orgasm diminishes performance anxiety in her partner and promotes higher self-esteem for both lovers. Have the confidence to expose and caress yourself. Men are natural voyeurs; they like to watch. Reveal your hidden pleasure spots, show your lover where to put his fingers, his tongue. Climax together. This releases the hormone for bonding. It is the same as breast feeding. Enhance your sex, evoke your sexual empowerment. Orgasms release endorphins. They make you happier and help you sleep better and live longer.

A true Goddess is a sexual being. Therein lays the secret.

"So sweet and delicious do I become, when I am in bed with a man who, I sense, loves and enjoys me, that the pleasure I bring excels all delight, so the knot of love, however tight it seemed before, is tied tighter still."[24]

These words, written by Veronica Franco (1546 – 1591), the most celebrated courtesan in Venice, show her infinite knowledge and great self-esteem, derived from her Goddess powers of love. Like generations of women before her, she was taught the intimate knowledge of men by her mother.

Unlike the married women of her time, being a courtesan in the most wanton city in Europe during the 1600s allowed her the freedom to educate and express herself. She became one of the most famous female poets of all time. Veronica Franco survived the Inquisition and provided a safe house for other courtesans facing the same charges.

"Phoebus, who serves the goddess of love,
and obtains from her as a sweet reward
what blesses him far more than being a god,
comes to reveal to my mind
the positions that Venus assumes with him
when she holds him in sweet embraces;
so that I, well taught in such matters,
know how to perform so well in bed
that this art exceeds Apollo's by far,
and my signing and writing are both forgotten
by the man who experiences me in this way,
which Venus reveals to people who serve her."[25]

Carrot Ribbons

Clean and wash carrots.
Cut off the ends and peel with a potato peeler.
Continue peeling the carrots, making long,
flat ribbons, until you have a good-sized bowl
of carrot strips. Add these few ingredients:
1 tablespoon of vinegar
1 teaspoon of fresh finely chopped Dill
1/2 teaspoon of rock salt
Combine all ingredients and leave to
marinate in the fridge for at least 1 to 2
hours before serving.

Carrots, Beans, and Asparagus

Delicious and divinely easy—carrots and beans
to die for. Zest them up, spice them up, and
make them taste great. Here's how!

Slice carrots into thin strips. Slice fresh yellow beans lengthways in half. Trim the
bottoms off the asparagus. Place vegetables in a foil pouch. Add fresh squeezed
lime, a tablespoon or so of butter, and lots of freshly cracked pepper. Close the
pouch and put it onto the fire, barbeque, or in the oven (at 375 degrees).
Cook until tender, about 20 minutes.

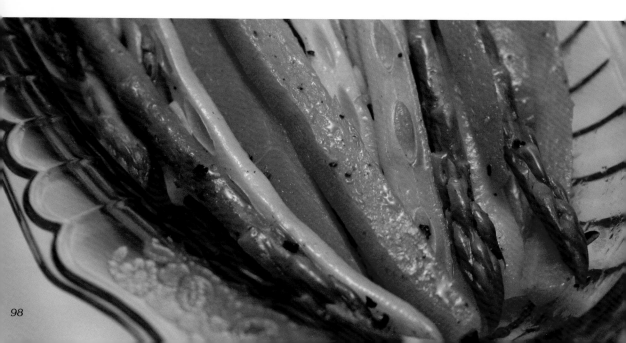

Peppers

Hundreds of species of chili peppers are grown throughout the world; some of the most common are the Habanero, Jalapeño, and Cayenne. These capsicum fruits contain twice the amount of vitamin C than citrus fruit and more vitamin A than all other vegetables, including carrots. They are a good source of folic acid, potassium, and vitamin E, great supporting for a healthy immune system.

The chemical capsaicin found in chilies produces a natural body heat that activates the release of endorphins, the same endorphins produced by the pituitary gland during orgasm. It is a natural neural stimulant (boosts metabolism) and analgesic (pain killer) that creates a feeling of well-being and pleasure. It is stimulating and, at the same time, relaxing. Capsaicin increases circulation, producing the energy to sweat and delivering the needed blood to the clitoris and penis, enabling both to become engorged to facilitate longer-lasting erections and hot, spirited orgasms.

Researchers discovered "cultivated chili starch grains"[26], which differ from "wild chili starch grains"[27], at archaeological sites in south western Ecuador, proving that chili peppers (Capsicum species) were farmed by ancient mankind 6100 years ago. Native to the Americas, with evidence of them found in prehistoric burial grounds from central southern Mexico to southern Peru, the pepper was taken from its birthplace to Spain in the late 1400s (with Christopher Columbus). It continued on to Asia and India, with the help of the Spanish and Portuguese explorers.

"The remains of these domesticated chili peppers were often found with corn . . ."[28]

Green Tomato Salsa

Dice 6 medium green tomatoes and 2 large red tomatoes. Chop fine and add to tomatoes: 1 medium onion, 5 cloves of fresh garlic, 1 bunch cilantro, and 3 fresh red or green hot peppers. Add the juice of 1 fresh lime and salt to taste. Stir and serve.

Salsa-Avocado Soup

Now that you have made the salsa, here is a soup recipe—good for colds, body aches, and respiratory problems. It is a body warming aphrodisiac for a cold winter night.

4 cups chicken broth either homemade or store-bought. 2 fresh tomatoes, diced. 1 1/2 cup salsa. 1 fresh, firm avocado. 1 fresh lime. Taco chips and salt to taste.

Pour chicken broth into a pot. Add fresh tomatoes and simmer 3 to 4 minutes until the tomatoes are tender. While broth is simmering, prepare the soup bowl. Cut an avocado in half, take out the seed, and scoop the avocado out of its skin into the bowl. Squeeze 1/2 fresh lime onto the avocado and add a dash of salt. Add salsa to the broth and simmer for 1 more minute. Pour your soup into the prepared bowl and top with a handful of taco chips. Serve immediately.

The Creole women of New Orleans, Louisiana (1700 – 1800), of mixed ancestry and varying skin colour, were the heirs of their French and Spanish foremothers; they were French speaking, Catholic, devoted to the Virgin Mary, and renowned for their beauty, social graces, and intelligence. The first women in America to do business, they were educated and cultured and had financial freedom, which was unheard of in the rest of the country. The had the right to own property, pursue a vocation and make their own will. They were the strength and bedrock of the Creole society in New Orleans (the word Creole means "native born").

These women were the most desired, sought-after paramours; hot-blooded, ardent lovers, passionate in their affairs and confident in their sexuality. New Orleans – The climate: Hot and humid. The diet: Fiery with spice, the heat from the chilies triggering a constant state of erotica . . . perspiring pheromones—the scent of sex, leaving the skin with a shiny glow, a silent communication inviting the thrill of intimacy.

Spirited Hot Chocolate

Seduce your lover with your scent, a seductive dance and a hot chocolate drink!

Melt dark chocolate in a saucepan with a vanilla bean. Pour into a cup, add brandy. Serve with 3 to 4 chili pepper seeds sprinkled lightly on top.

Create some body heat of your own with herb-garlic prawns, barbequed
to perfection, and drizzled with chili/Vodka/marmalade glaze.

Freshly shelled prawn tails: Slice along the back, in the centre of the tail, and
discard the vein as you rinse the shrimp. In a small saucepan, melt 1 heaping
tablespoon of butter with 1 clove of crushed garlic. Add 1/2 teaspoon each dried
Basil, Oregano, and crushed Rosemary. Skewer the prawns and baste with the
butter/herb mixture. Barbeque 3 to 5 minutes, add a pinch of rock salt, serve with
glaze drizzled on top. Glaze: melted lime marmalade with dried chilies and Vodka.

Vegetable Kingdom Stuffed Peppers

This recipe comes from mythical Greece. It calls for enough rice/vegetable stuffing and sauce to fill 8 small peppers. This is a delicate dish with the combination of different tastes in every bite—the peppers, rice, vegetables, and sauce. We are going to start with the rice.

Take 3 cups of slightly undercooked rice and let cool. Chop into small pieces: 1/2 medium onion, 3 cloves of garlic, 3 small celery stalks with leafy tops, 1/2 medium potatoe, 1/2 small sweet potatoe—peeled, 2 small parsnips—peeled, 1 large broccoli stalk—peeled, 2 medium carrots, 3 cauliflower pieces, 1/2 zucchini, 15 green beans.

In a large frypan, heat 3 tablespoons of grapeseed oil and 1 to 1 1/2 teaspoons butter to the sizzle point. Add the onions, garlic, and celery first; the hard-root vegetables and the zucchini and beans last.

Add spices: 2 teaspoons Oregano, 2 teaspoons Basil, 1/2 teaspoon Thyme. Salt and pepper to taste.

Sauté until vegetables begin to soften. Let cool. Mix with cooled rice (you want approximately 2 cups of sautéd vegetables to each 3 cups of cooked rice). Let sit while you make the sauce.

Now the sauce:
1 1/2 medium Onions, 6 cloves garlic, 16 small-medium roma tomatoes, 2 teaspoons Rosemary, 2 teaspoons Basil. Salt and Pepper to taste.

Sauté onions and garlic in tablespoons of grapeseed oil and 1 teaspoon butter. (Butter is optional. Just add a bit more oil.) Chop tomatoes and add to pan. Add spices and let simmer for 3/4 hour.

Cut a lid into the pepper around the stem and slice the seeds and excess pulp off its underside. Gently scoop out anything left inside. Trim the stem. Stuff the raw peppers with the vegetable/rice mixture, put the lid back on, and place into a baking dish. Pour the tomato sauce over the peppers (your sauce should almost come to the top of the peppers in the dish). Cover with foil, leaving the sides slightly open as a steam vent; bake at 350 degrees for 1 hour.

Exotic Lentil Soup

We don't want to soak our lentils anymore or make chicken broth every time we want to make soup, so here is an incredible soup recipe that can be simmering in the pot within 25 minutes.

Vigorous and stimulating, with all of the spices that enjoy a history of aphrodisiac lore, this soup kindles a slow, rousing heat.

Pour 1/4 cup grapeseed oil into the bottom of a pot.

Add: 1/2 large onion—diced, 1 large carrot, 3 potatoes—cut into large cubes, 1/2 cup green onion, 1 celery stick—chopped fine. Fry for 10 minutes

Add: 2 cups of water—simmer with lid on for 10 minutes, 1 - 900 ml. box of chicken broth—simmer with lid on for 10 minutes, 2 teaspoons of Knorr chicken broth. Mix with 3 more cups of water

Add: 2 teaspoons of creamed coconut or 1/2 cup of coconut milk. 1 cup of plain yogurt, and 4 cans of lentils.

Blend: 1/2 teaspoon of each spice into a bowl, then pour these spices into the pot: Coriander, Turmeric, red Chili powder, Cumin, Clove, black peppercorn, Ginger powder, Cardamom, and Cinnamon. Salt and pepper to taste.

Simmer soup for 3/4 hour. Add 1 cup of frozen peas 15 minutes before serving. If the broth boils down too much, add water—1/2 cup at a time. Salt and pepper to taste

History of Fruit

One of the early cultivated foods in the world was fruit, with evidence of fruit crops in Egypt dating back to 10,000 BCE. During the Bronze Age, between 6000 to 3000 BCE, nomadic hunter-foragers evolved into civilized societies through husbandry of the land and irrigation of the water.

The first propagated orchards in the Mediterranean consisted of the grapevine,the date, and fig and pomegranate trees. Theophrastus (371 – 287 BCE)—the "Father of Botany"—Aristotle's heir, who inherited his written works and lavish personal gardens, gives technical depictions on the art of grafting and artificial pollinating of these ancient trees and vines. The quince (thought to be the *apple* from the Garden of Paradise) pear, plum, and citrus fruits took their origin from Central and East Asia.

"Chloris approached
the landscape flew!
All nature vanish'd from my view!
She seem'd all nature to comprize
Her lips! her beauteous breasts! her eyes!
That rous'd and yet abash'd desire,
With liquid, languid, living fire!"[29]

"Zephyros: The son of Astraeus and of Eros, he was the personification of the West Wind which brings with it freshness and rain in the spring. He would unite with Chloris, goddess of the new vegetation, from which would sprout the fresh fruits of the soil."[30] Zephyros and Chloris produced a son, Carpus, which means fruit in Ancient Greek.

The worship of natural phenomena, especially the coming of spring—the renewal of life on Earth—was essential in myriad early religions; among the most sacred rites was the supplication of fruit to the Mother Earth incarnate, the Goddess. One of the earliest illustrated works of art in history, the Uruk vase, depicts the Sumerian King Dumuzi presenting the Goddess Inanna, a female in human form, her crown—a horned headdress, with offerings of baskets overflowing with fruit, vegetables, and grain—a testimonial of crop cultivation from as early as 3000 BCE.

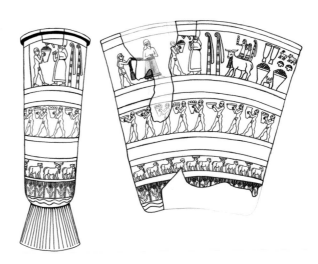

"One of a large number of terracotta images of lovers on beds found in Mesopotamia. Often understood as connected to the "Sacred Marriage" rite, with the woman seen as a "sacred prostitute." Dated to the third millennium BCE."[31]

"Ninshubur, the faithful servant of the holy shrine of Uruk,
Led Dumuzi to the sweet thighs of Inanna and spoke."[32]

"My queen, here is the choice of your heart,
The king, your beloved bridegroom.
May he spend long days in the sweetness of your holy loins.
Give him a favorable and glorious reign."[33]

Inanna speaks . . .

*"He shaped my loins with his fair hands,
The shepherd Dumuzi filled my lap with cream and milk,
He stroked my pubic hair,
He watered my womb.
He laid his hands on my holy vulva,
He smoothed my black boat with cream,
He quickened my narrow boat with milk,
He caressed me on the bed.*

*"Now I will caress my high priest on the bed,
I will caress the faithful shepherd Dumuzi,
I will caress his loins, the shepherdship of the land,
I will decree a sweet fate for him."*

*"My beloved, the delight of my eyes, met me.
We rejoiced together.
He took his pleasure of me.
He brought me into his house.*

*"He laid me down on the fragrant honey-bed.
My sweet love, lying by my heart,
Tongue-playing, one by one,
My fair Dumuzi did so fifty times.*

"Now, my sweet love is sated." [34]

The Hieros Gamos—a sacred sex ritual, open to the view of all—where the Heirodule or Priestess would embody the deity of the Goddess and couple with the King and by their union, guarantee fertile abundance for their country and its people. This ceremony was first documented in early Sumeria, one of the foremost civilizations of the world (3000 BCE), depicting Inanna and Dumuzi, showing the Goddess's acceptance of Dumuzi as ruler by gifting him "shepherdship" of the land.

Numerous pagan sects in history celebrated the ceremonial act of Hieros Gamos. In ancient Britain it was heralded as the Great Rite, observed on Beltaine eve, where man and woman would incarnate God and Goddess and bestow an offering of fertility to Mother Earth.

God Jupiter and Goddess Juno enacting the *Hieros Gamos*

The Plum

In the *Book of Songs*, the foremost existing collection of Chinese poetry, believed to be assembled by the Chinese philosopher and teacher Confucius (551 – 479 BCE), many writings give praise to the plum and the plum blossom, their beauty captured and kept for eternity in the silk embroidery of the Emperors. The plum tree, first to blossom in spring—the season of amorous awakening for the Earth—bears the plum, a renowned aphrodisiac heralding from antiquity.

The plum ignites the pleasure senses of the body by increasing vitality with its natural sugar and high iron, potassium, magnesium and vitamin A content. It promotes digestive health, detoxifies the body, and cleanses the blood, giving the skin a rosy appeal, increasing energy and rousing the mood for romance.

"Fruit plummets from the plum tree
but seven of ten plums remain.
You gentlemen who would court me,
come on a lucky day.
Fruit plummets from the plum tree
but three of ten plums still remain.
You men who want to court me,
come now, today is a lucky day!
Fruit plummets from the plum tree.
You can fill up your baskets.
Gentlemen if you want to court me,
just say the word."[35]

Book of Songs (circa 600 BCE)

Behind Every Great Man, There Stands A Great Woman

Alexander the Great (356 – 320 BCE), while conquering the Persian Empire, discovered the plum and sent it back to the Mediterranean. From there it found its way throughout Europe.

Alexander had numerous passionate love affairs and more than one wife. It took a very special woman to champion his many lovers, one bestowed with heart-stirring powers of seduction. Roxana, (*Little Star*, in her native tongue) a Bactrian Princess, was that woman. Alexander was so impassioned with his love for her that he stood against the will of the Macedonians who wanted him to marry a princess of the blood (a true Macedonian), and took Roxana for his wife and queen. Their marriage encouraged collaboration between the Greek and Eastern cultures that exists to this day. Roxana became pregnant but Alexander did not see his son and heir to the throne. He died before his son was born.

Plum Bums

Preserved with the energy and warmth of the sun—each plum, a banquet of flavour, a warming infusion of gentle excitement erupting with every bite. Feast upon the plums and sip the elixir.

Wash the plums and pierce the skin with a toothpick (2 to 3 holes). This allows the alcohol to penetrate the plum. Place the plums in a clean jar (scald, using boiling water) with a sealable lid. Add brown sugar (the sugar you pour in depends on the size of the jar; we usually use enough to fill 1/4 of the jar), whole 3 to 5 whole Cloves, and 1 whole Nutmeg. Add enough brandy to fill up the jar to the top. Tightly close the jar and place in the sun until the sugar dissolves (1 to 2 weeks), turning the jar every few days. Store in a cool, dark place until you are ready to open it.

The Cherry

"First cherry blossoms,
a cuckoo, the moon and snow:
another year closes"[36]

The momentary, fleeting beauty of cherry blossoms, the arresting seductiveness of viewing the delicate flowers parallel the sexual allure of the Japanese courtesan and the brief visits to the *pleasure quarters*.

In the morning, like the blossoms, the night pleasures vanish, the bitter-sweet memory of the liaison lingers, captivated in Ukiyo-e (pictures of the *floating world*), the Shunga wood block prints of the Edo period (1615 – 1868).

Courtesans of Daimonjiya
Viewing Cherry Blossoms

Like the butterfly from the cocoon, cherry blossom viewing—Sakuro—a 2000-year-old custom—hails the passage of the seasons from winter to spring. As shown in the image above, the Japanese courtesan did not wear the traditional foot covering, the tabi, but preferred to reveal a whisper of bare flesh peeking out from under the folds of her kimono.

The Japanese courtesan is the honoured ancestress of the geisha, the most accomplished and the most beautiful. At the top of the hierarchy of courtesans, the Tayuu refined the artistry of carnal knowledge with their expertise in sexual intimacy. Living in the realm of femininity, they passed on their knowledge to young apprentices—Kamuro—who in turn served and learned the skills of the courtesan. Valued for their learned minds; their art of conversation, music, and poetry; the beauty of their dress; and the ability to define and understand the world of men, the Tayuu were true entertainers, but their real knowledge was the ancient wisdom of pleasuring a man. This rigorous training entailed seduction, massage, sexual positions and games, bathing erotica, masturbation, breathing techniques, oral sex, and penis play.

The written ancestry of the cherry heralds from as far back as 300 BCE and has been touted as an aphrodisiac ever since. It has been affiliated with the loss of virginity and sexual innocence since antiquity, the seed symbolizing the uterus, and the juice, the blood. Rich in vitamins and minerals—potassium, calcium, iron, and vitamins C, A, and E—they also contain high levels of melatonin that calm the mind and nervous system, thus promoting sleep. The cherry boosts your immune system and makes you feel relaxed and rejuvenated. Comprised of anti-inflammatory and analgesic (pain relief) attributes with blood-alkalizing properties, cherries offer you an all-around feeling of well-being.

Cherry Bombs

Take as many ripe cherries as can fit into a canning jar. Sterilize the jar (see page #175) and clean and remove the stems from the cherries. With a toothpick, pierce the butt end of the cherry, sliding the toothpick into both sides, to enable full absorption the alcohol. Layer the cherries into the jar with the stemless end up to catch the sugar as it falls through to the bottom. Make sure they are snug; the more cherries, the more fun! After every 2 layers of fruit, add 2 tablespoons of sugar. Add 1 cinnamon stick for extra taste. Gently pour vodka into the jar, covering the cherries. Leave 1/4 inch of space at the top of the jar.

Place in a sunny spot, indoors or outdoors, for 1 week, turning the jars to expose a new side to the sun every 2 to 3 days; the sun seals the jar and melts the sugar, infusing the cherries with spice and spirits. The vodka takes on the taste of the cherries.

Eat the cherries . . . create a cordial liqueur by adding the cherry and spice liqueur to champagne, white wine, or sparkling water.

Blackberry & Raspberry

The "First Nations" women of the Americas taught the early settlers the age-old skills of preserving berries—blackberries, raspberries, and other wild berries—by drying them in the sun to supplement their diet for the coming winter. Brewed as tea, baked in breads (bannic and cornbread), pounded into pemmican (meat, dried fruit, and suet), eaten as a treat: fresh-picked or sun-dried, added to water to make a sweet refreshing drink or used as medicine, these berries were truly valued among the hunter-gatherer nations.

There is physical evidence showing the blackberry in the diet of the "first peoples" from Europe, dating as far back as 2500 years ago; using radio-carbon-dating, the death of the "Haraldskær Woman," an "Iron Age" woman (8th century BCE to 6th century BCE) revealed in 1835 in Jutland, Denmark, was dated circa 500 BCE. Forensic analysis revealed blackberries in her stomach. The tannins in the peat bog where she was discovered created a natural preservative, curing her skeleton, skin, internal organs, and the contents of her stomach.

Used in the folkways of worship for spell craft, protection, and health-giving in one of the oldest Pagan religions in history, the riotous wild Blackberry was hallowed as a spiritual plant kindred to the Irish deity Brigit. Heralding from Celtic Eire (the ancient name for Ireland) Brigit or Brighid—daughter of Dagda, descendant of the Tuatha de Danaan, ancestral Faerie people of Ireland—is a Goddess of three faces: Poetry, wisdom and shamanism; the mysticism of the Druid long song; transformation and enlightenment; Leechcraft, intuition, healing, and fertility; and Metalsmithing, the flame and cauldron, magic, foreknowledge, second sight.

To bring the Celtic people to Christianity, the Church named the Goddess Brigit a Saint. They built one of the first Christian convents, Kildare Abbey, on the site of her sacred shrine, enfolding the Priestesses who tended her fire and holy wells into the nunnery and naming Brigit—namesake of the Goddess and daughter of a Druid—Abbess (453 – 524 AD). The original Abbey is said to have been destroyed in the twelfth century AD.

"The spear, mural crown, and globe represent Brigantia's protection of the tribe"[37]

"According to the legend of the Irish Saint Bride she was transported miraculously to Bethlehem to attend the nativity of Christ. Here two angels carry the white robed saint across the sea."[38]

119

Known as Bride in Scotland, Brigantia in Britain, and Brigandu in Gaul, the Goddess of Smithcraft, Fire, and the Cauldron is celebrated on her feast day Imbolc (February 1), the first spring festival of the Pagan calendar. People would rejoice the renewal of life, symbolized by the smothering and re-lighting of the hearth fire—this represented the rising sun and the warmth of the coming spring. A perpetual flame, enshrined and tended first by Priestesses at her temple in Kildara, Ireland, then, for over 1000 years, by the Brighidine nuns at the Abbey of St. Brigit of Kildare, was kept burning until the early 1200s, then re-lit and brought back to life in 1993.

Light a sacred flame—a living force, an offering—to welcome the Goddess Brigit. The flames cast a vision, a summons to the Universe, a doorway to second sight. Offer a libation to the fire; drink (of the Blackberry Elixir) and enter a trance-like state of consciousness. Gaze upon the fire and visualize the light of the flames warming the breath of the aura around your living self. Recite your incantation, they are your words of power (see page #171).

Become mesmerized by the life force of the fire, the hypnotic effect of the flames, the vital spark of the elixir as it opens a rift to the supernatural. The spirit answer comes to you when you relax and ponder the question, inviting premonition and intuition . . . divining by fire.

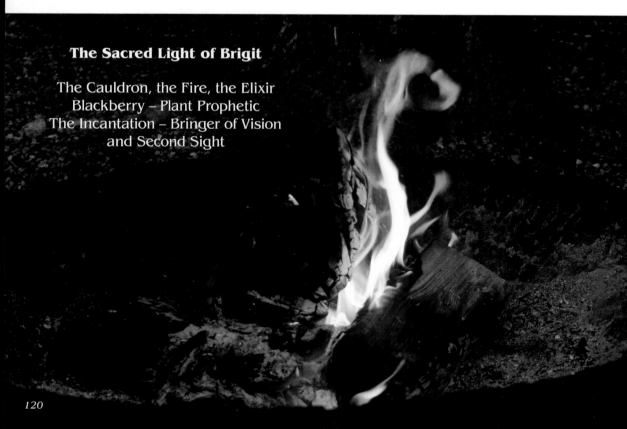

The Sacred Light of Brigit

The Cauldron, the Fire, the Elixir
Blackberry – Plant Prophetic
The Incantation – Bringer of Vision
and Second Sight

Blackberry Elixir
Blackberries, Vodka, Sugar

If you don't have a place to light a fire, a fireplace in your home or firepit in your backyard, you can use five candles arranged in a small circle placed on a table in front of you, to symbolize the 5-point Neopagan Goddess Star (see page 14).

Recipes for medicinal use of the blackberry fruit, bark, and leaf have been penned in books of herbals, folk medicine, and home remedies throughout Europe and Britain for over 2000 years. A tea brewed from the bark was used to treat dysentry and diarrhea; the astringent leaf tea for comfort of sore throat, bleeding gums, cankerous mouth sores, oily or infected skin, and insect bites. The fresh berry—high in vitamin C, iron, folate, calcium, magnesium, and potassium—was made into a tonic and prescribed for malaise and iron loss in women It has anti-oxidant, anti-viral and anti-bacterial properties and is a blood-builder and cleanser. Blackberries contain pain-relieving and blood-thinning salicylates—substances found in aspirin.

??Within a lily? Centre placed???
Or ever marked the pretty beam
A strawberry shows half drowned in cream?
Or seen rich rubies blushing through
A pure smooth pearl, and orient too?
So like to this, nay all the rest,
Is each neat niplet of her breast."[39]

Women's breasts have brought pleasure to men just by beholding them; they have
been written about in poems, sung to, dreamed of, and longed for since time
immemorial. Two of the most famous breasts in *herstory* belonged to Agnes Sorel.

Agnes Sorel (1421 – 1450) was the first mistress of a French King to be acknowledged by the royal court—hers was the first face of a royal mistress on canvas (her lover, King Charles VII of France, had her face painted on the Madonna, baring her perfect breast, holding the baby Jesus). Her self-esteem was so great, her position of power so assured (Charles was infatuated with her) that she was able to create the daring fashionable trend in dress at the court of baring her breast—a gift of pleasure and symbol of female sexuality.

"In a recess adorned, which met the gaze, Neither obscure, nor filled by splendid rays, Between two rich embroidered sheets were laid The dazzling beauties of the heavenly maid. Near the alcove a portal open stood, Which gentle Alix, dame expert and good, The chamber quitting never thought to close. O! You in whose soft breasts the passion glows, Lovers, 'tis you can feel the sharp desire, The strong impatience of great Gallia's sire. The graceful tresses that adorned his head, Already were with choicest perfumed spread, He came! O! Tender moment, blissful night, He sprang towards his mistress with delight! Quick throbbed their hearts; both tender love and shame The cheek of Agnes tinged with roseate flame; But bashfulness soon fled; the lover's arms Banished all fears, save tender love's alarms; Dazzled, enchanted were his ardent eyes, That wildly gazed upon the heavenly prize: Who but would worship, that like him had pressed A neck in fairest alabaster dressed; Two rising orbs at equal distance placed, Heaving and falling, by Love's pencil traced, Each crowned with vermil blood of damask rose; Enchanting bosom which ne'er knew repose, You seemed the gaze and pressure to invite, And wooed the longing lips to seek delight."[40]

Blackberry Booby Trap – A Body Syrup

A *Tease Tincture* aphrodisiac . . . transcendent sweet indulgence, inviting the tongue; licking, lingering, the pursed lips pulling, caressing . . . tender love bites on the hardened nipples, waves of butterfly pleasure fluttering through your inner sex, awakening your natural lubricant—desirous—your clitoris pulsating with the foretaste of orgasm—hot, wet sex play.

A man's nipple is equally as sensitive as a woman's. To intensify your partner's sexual arousal, try stimulating his nipples, some like it; some don't. Be gentle to begin with.

Making love to the breast has a powerful effect on a woman's body—a pampering part of intimacy and foreplay, to pay divine honour to the total woman. The seductive secrets coveted by women of the night—the arts of pleasuring: The courtesan . . . fondling, squeezing, tweaking her own nipples, triggering arousal.

Be high spirited, have fun, seize the moment. Elicit his lust with a private peep show, the cupless bra with a pert nipple. Touch yourself, show your lover what you want, adorn your breasts in body syrup. Present them to your paramour. Squeeze his penis between your syrupy breasts, and in turn, receive the ultimate *pearl necklace*.

Red Raspberry Cordial

Mix this cordial with sparkling water, crushed ice, and a squeeze of lime for a hot summer afternoon. Indulge in adult time with champagne or the spirits of your choice.

De-stem and wash ripe berries. Let dry on a clean towel. Sterilize jar with boiling water. Place berries in the jar adding 2 tablespoons of sugar for every 2 layers of berries. Cold-infuse in the fridge for 3 to 4 days until the sugar dissolves into a syrup.

Because of the Antimicrobial properties of the raspberry juice, this remedial tonic—passed down through generations—is used to reduce the symptoms of food poisoning.

Raspberry Leaf Tea

Tea brewing: Hunting wild plants, scavenging the back yard garden for fruits and their leaves, growing and gathering herbs and flowers, drying and creating an infinite number of hexing and vexing blends—a medley of magic to infuse into a tea.

Raspberry Leaf Tea: This long-standing folk remedy was valued by women healers of nomadic people from the northern hemisphere of our world for thousands of years. The Native Americans and European Gypsies were well acquainted with the raspberry plant and understood the curative benefits of the leaf when brewed into a tea. It was introduced to young girls as a ritual for their coming of age, it helps expectant mothers with birthing, and enriches and enlivens a woman's libido as she ages.

Potent, vital to a woman's sensualism, this tea tones and soothes your inner pelvic muscles and soft tissues, awakening your flower of sexuality and increasing your romantic appetite. It is an all round youth serum for hair, bones, teeth, and skin, fine-tuning the harmony of a woman's metabolism (PMS and hot flashes).

Raspberry Leaf brewed into tea and partaken before meeting your lover can turn a mediocre date into a hot, wet, sexy night to remember, full of orgasmic pleasure, gifting you with dream visions into the night.

Raspberry leaf tea is high in such minerals as iron, calcium, magnesium, phosphorus, and potassium. It is rich in vitamins C, E, A, and B-complex. Used as a rinse, it heals the soft tissue in the mouth and the vagina, preparing you for love, and healing you after having too much fun.

Raspberry Sex Tonic

Simmer together: 1 cup fresh berries, 1 cup water, 2 tablespoons honey. Steep: 2 large tablespoons of dried raspberry leaves (in the spring, collect the new shoots), 1 teaspoon dried Lavender. Add raspberry-honey mixture to the tea. Serve hot or cold.

The Strawberry

Nothing declares romantic intentions like the strawberry . . . shaped like a heart, endowed with the colour of deep red lips and blessed with the sweet perfume of sexuality (the Latin name for strawberries is *Fragaria*, which means fragrance.) This potent love berry was chosen, above all other fruit, as the symbol for Venus, the Goddess of Love.

And rightly so . . . the mouth-watering delight, the hedonic thrill of biting into the heart of the berry, the juice and flavour exploding onto your taste buds assails your senses with the piquancy and aroma of shameless thoughts and wanton desires.

The Strawberry Kiss . . . pursuing affairs of the heart, fresh—sweet and succulent —the scent of seduction. The eroticism of feeding fruit to your sweetheart by hand, stroking fingers with your tongue, caressing with your lips, mouth to mouth — fevered with pleasure. Strawberry —the *fruit nipple*. Purse it between your lips and offer a bite to your lover.

"The moth's kiss, first!
Kiss me as if you made me believe
You were not sure, this eve,
How my face, your flower, had pursed
Its petals up; so, here and there
You brush it, till I grow aware
Who wants me, and wide open I burst."[41]

The 18th century French courtesan Madam Tallien (1773 – 1835) loved to bathe in mashed strawberries as a beauty essence, an elixir of youth. (Strawberries have alpha-hydroxy acid, which exfoliates dead skin cells.) Acclaimed for displaying her nude body through diaphanous gauze and transparent silk, Madame Tallien seduced some of the most powerful men of the period—the Marquess de Fontenay; the Jacobin, Tallien; Barras, the head of the Directory; the millionaire Ouvrad; and ultimately, the Prince of Chimay. Her renowned parlour, the most influential salon during the French Revolution, became the centre of Directoire society, where the influential met to discuss politics and current affairs, analyze philosophical and literary ideas, establish connections, and promote self-advancement.

— ci-devant Occupations :_ or _ Madame Talian and the Empress Josephine dancing Naked before Barrass in the Winter of 1797._ A Fact !
Barrass (then in Power) being tond of Josephine, promised Buonaparte, a promotion, on condition that he would take her off his hands ;—Barrass had as usual, drank freely, & placed Buonaparte behind a Screen, while he amused himself with these two Ladies, who were then his humble dependants._Madame Talian is a beautiful Woman, tall & elegant; Josephine is smaller & thin, with bad Teeth, something like Cloves,_ it is needless to add that Buonaparte accepted the Promotion & the Lady,_ now, Empress of France.

The salons of Theresa Cabarrus (Madame Tallien) had an enormous influence on the European world; not only did she intervene (along with Josephine de Beauharnais—Josephine Bonaparte) and save countless people from the guillotine, she was one of the primary influences on the famous love affair and subsequent marriage of Josephine to Napoleon Bonaparte (Napoleon was introduced to Josephine, his "lucky star," at one of her soirées).

Being social animals, we thrive on companionship and interaction with other people. To become less isolated, it is important to plan and entertain social gatherings, introducing atmosphere and conversation, good food, merriment, and the opportunity to flirt. Involve your friends; have a modern-day parlour.

Madame Tallien, the notorious coquette and salonniere, entertained her prominent guests with the best French cuisine and spirits, crafting the artistry of social life during the most alive period in France's history. For diversion and amusement, music and parlour games —card playing, chess, poetry reading, short plays, all vibrant with a sexual undercurrent—provided the opportunity for her guests to meet their lovers and arrange secret liaisons. The memory of a stolen kiss, an intimate caress, an urgent embrace yearning for release, lingers on . . . until the next rendezvous.

Strawberry-Lavender Wine
Liqueur soaked strawberries and the age-old magic of Lavender elevate the wine to a higher levelof euphoric bliss, rousing the spirits of everyone who partakes.

Euphoric Enchantment: An Old World Drink ~ Strawberry-Lavender Wine
Wine – Pinot Gris or White Zinfandal
1/2 cup liqueur-infused dried strawberries
2 tablespoons dried lavender
Drop the dried strawberries and lavender into the bottom of your decanter. Fill with wine and cold-infuse in the fridge overnight. This wine is enchanting with or without the strawberries.

The Fine Art of Drying Strawberries

~ Prepare the strawberries (wash, dry, pluck stems).
~ Soak them in strawberry liqueur for 3 to 4 hours; this adds a wonderful taste and helps preserve the colour.
~ Place the strawberries on 2 layers of parchment paper on a cookie sheet and place in the sun (on a hot sunny day) or in the oven at the lowest setting (160 degrees or less), with the door ajar.

The key to drying fruit is adequate air flow. If you are drying the fruit in the sun, pick a spot with a breeze or position a fan near the drying trays. Drying strawberries in the sun can take up to 3 days. Bring inside at the end of the hottest part of the late afternoon.

If you use the oven, place a fan on a stool in front of the open oven door. Turn the fan on a low setting and turn the fruit every few hours. After the berries are dry enough to handle, string with a needle and thread and hang in a dry, airy place (not in the kitchen because of the steam and food fumes). Store in a glass jar.

"Wife, into the garden and set me a plot
With strawberry roots, the best to be got;
Such growing abroad among thorns in the wood,
Well chosen and picked, prove excellent good."[42]

The wild strawberry, prized for its sweet and flavourful taste, was carried home from the woodland and transplanted into the garden to become the domesticated strawberry of today. This tiny, fragrant plant soon journeyed from a favoured food delicacy to a remedy, due to its wealth of curative properties. It provides relief for digestive upset and has pain-relieving effects (it's an anti-inflammatory), blood-building and cleansing effects, too—(anti-oxidants and iron). It helps maintain a healthy immune system (zinc, folic acid, and vitamin C), promotes oral health, and restores and maintains healthy skin (fruit acid and high vitamin C content).

Strawberry Leaf Tea: This tea is mild and soothing to an upset stomach caused by diarrhea, liver complaints, or heavy periods. Dry strawberry leaves and infuse with boiling water. Wrap the teapot with a towel to keep it hot and let steep for 5 minutes. For a fruity flavour, add strawberries to the brew.

The Morning-After Strawberry Cornbread

1 cup cream-style corn
1 cup sour cream
3 eggs
1/3 cup corn oil
1 1/2 teaspoon baking powder
1/2 teaspoon salt
1 cup cornmeal
1 cup liqueur, infused
dried strawberries

Combine ingredients together in a medium-sized bowl. With a wooden spoon, stir until completely blended. Pour into a well-greased cast iron pan (a bread pan will do). Bake in a preheated oven at 350 degrees for about 30 minutes or until the bread pulls away from the side of the pan and has a nice bounce when pressed lightly in the centre. Serve hot with butter and honey.

The Magic Apple

For thousands of years the apple has been at the centre of mythology and magic, for both seduction and fertility rites as far back as the story of Adam and Eve. Cultivated in the gardens of Paradise, at the heart of such timeless tales as Avalon, Island of the Apples, and home of Morgan le Fay—Defender of the Goddess Faith, the apple has been considered sacred and thought to possess the secret of eternal youth.

MORGAN LE FAY CASTS AWAY THE SCABBARD

The apple's otherworldly presence is recounted in many civilizations: In Greek mythology, the Goddess Gaia (Mother Earth) presents Hera, Celestial Queen, with an apple tree for a wedding present when she marries Zeus, King of the Olympian Gods. Tended by the Hesperides—wood nymphs charged with guarding the tree —the golden apples bestowed everlasting life.

"All amid the Gardens fair
Of Hesperus and his daughters three
That sing about the golden tree."[43]

In 43 AD, the Romans conquered the Celts and combined the ancient Celtic festival Samhain with a festival honouring the harvest and Pomona, Goddess of Fruit and Trees. Entwined with abundance and fertility, her regalia, the apple. She is celebrated on the night the dead walk the earth with the living.

In Folklore, the apple Tree was the favourite home of the Faerie Queen, steeped in enchantment and legend. Those unfortunate mortals who lingered too long under a fruit-laden bough could be carried off to Faerie land, sometimes never to return.

The apple represents women's power and sexuality, depending on which way it is cut, either lying down—revealing a woman's reproductive system, or standing up—the magical symbol of the 5-pointed star, the pentagram.

Hard Apple Cider, a known aphrodisiac since its discovery, (first recorded in 55 BCE by the Romans when they arrived in Britain), has long been the favourite drink before bedding down, the intermediate amatorial between the dinner table and the sheets. Rich in vitamins and minerals, it bestows a healthy glow to the whole body, assailing the libido and arousing sexual fervour.

Wassail, a long-established celebration on the Old Twelfth Night (January 17) in honour of the Goddess Pomona to embolden the harvest. The offering is pieces of toast dipped in cider and placed in the forks of the trees to rally the birds. The cider is then poured onto the roots of the trees.

Apple Tree Spirit Smudge

In the Goddess and Druid faith of the British Isles, never was a live branch taken off an apple tree unless it was used for magic, and then, proper thanks were given, for the whole tree was considered sacred. Only the pruned branches or sucker shoots were used so as not to bring harm to the tree.

When doing spells that require apple bark and wood, gather the cut branches from a recently pruned apple tree; the tree is invigorated and happy to be tended, making the spell more potent. (Prune during winter, when the tree is dormant.) Hang the branches and dry them over time in a dark, airy place to preserve the magical influence of the tree.

Love Unrequited: Call Upon the Apple Bark

This smudge heralds the healing of a broken heart. The dried wood from the apple tree invokes an alchemic evolution from negative to positive. Light 1 to 2 charcoal tablets (depending on the size of smudge you want) or retrieve a burning coal from your fireplace and place it in the bottom of your metal smudge pot or shell. Once the coal is lit, place small twigs or shavings onto the coal and let them smoke. If they ignite, gently blow out the fire so it will smoke instead of burn.

Envelop yourself in the halo of smoke. As the smudge is being delivered, envision your heart becoming whole again. Feel the change of energy surrounding you, a conjuration of light delivering a message of peace to you and your environment. Here is an incantation we have used.

**Love Unrequited Heal my Heart,
Spirit Chaser of the Apple Bark
Hear My Call, I Summon Thee
Release My Sorrow and Set it Free**

Once we have finished, we Give Thanks to the Universe and the Spirit of the Apple Tree.

Sugarless Applesauce

~ Clean, core, and peel your apples.
~ Clean and prepare your strawberries.
~ If you have pears, do the same
  adding pears makes this concoction
  even sweeter).
~ You want to have double the
  amount of apples as strawberries.
~ If you add pears, cut down the
  amount of apples.

Place fruit into a pot, leaving enough space at the top for the fruit to swell as it cooks. Add water to cover 1/3 of the fruit. Bring to a boil, then simmer with the lid on for 1 hour or until the fruit is cooked to the consistency you like.

This sauce can be served alone or can accompany pork, potato pancakes, and cereal, or can be used in recipes like banana bread or muffins instead of sugar.

The Medicine Apple

An oldfashioned remedy for diarrhea or *foul stomach*.
Take 1 apple, 2 if you like—wash, peel, and core—grate onto a plate and leave in a pile for 20 minutes. Once the apple has turned brown, eat it.

Apple Honey

This is a wonderful little recipe to perk up your morning.
Serve with everything from simple toast to muffins and yogurt.

Peel and core 12 apples and put them in a medium-size pot. Add 1 cup of apple cider and 4 teaspoons of honey. At this point, you can add spice if you like—Cinnamon, Allspice, Nutmeg, or Cloves to taste. Simmer for 30 minutes or until you get the consistency you want.

Apple

Stuffed Chicken

With this recipe, you can take a chicken from the bag to the roaster—with gravy drippings to anticipate—in 20 to 25 minutes.

~ Wash the chicken. (Remove the giblets—liver, heart, gizzard.) Wash and core 2 to 3 apples, depending on the size of the chicken.

~ Peel 1 large onion and 3 large cloves of garlic.

~ Slice and mix together the apples, onions, and garlic.

~ Rub a generous amount of olive oil with a tablespoon of rock salt on the chicken.

Now, stuff the chicken with the apple/onion/garlic mixture and place in your roasting pan. Rub olive oil on the bottom of the pan so it washes easier at the end of the day.

For a nice savoury taste, sprinkle the chicken with a generous amount of herbs: Oregano, Rosemary, Basil, and Thyme, allowing some herbs to fall into the bottom of the pan. This makes an excellent gravy. Add a spattering of pepper to top it off.

Put 1/2 cup of water and 2 sun-dried tomatoes into the bottom of the pan. Bake covered at 400 degrees for the first 1/2 hour, then uncover and continue baking at 350 degrees, 20 minutes per pound.

GARDEN ALCHEMY

"Every Flower was the Emblem of a God;
Every Tree the Abode of a Nymph"[44]

"Garden Goddess
Come to mine
In that special
Evening time
Sun sinking low
With moon in sight
Bless my Garden
Before the night"[45]

145

Garden Alchemy

Garden Alchemy is the actualization of the gifts from the garden, the manifestation of the magic in the plants—planning ahead, planting herbs with the alchemy of harvest in your mind's eye . . . envisioning the leaves and flowers of the Rosemary, Basil, Oregano, and Lavender throughout the summer and fall.

Your garden is where you learn to tend the lifeblood and the heart of the Earth. By not growing and harvesting our own food, we have lost touch with Mother Nature and the rituals surrounding the planting, harvesting, and preparation of food.

Every animal, plant, rock, and stream has its own life force or spirit. A Blessing or an Offering of Thanks should be given before harvesting or using Earth essence. These blessings are most important because they alter and improve the quality of that which is blessed. This blessing should contain a Charm ordained for the use of the plant—a prayer or poem to restore life so that others may grow in its place—a Spiritual Communication to the Goddess, the Earth Mother.

Throughout the weave of time, women, the foragers and gatherers, discovered the mysteries of the Great Mother, Earth. First they harvested the wealth of the forest, than learned the secrets of gardening, collecting the seed and cultivating plants. Recorded in story and song, the pathway of knowledge was passed down from woman to woman for generations. This instruction opened the portal of enlightenment to medicinal nurturing; women were the natural mid-wives and healers, working in the still room, harnessing the energy of each plant, learning to dry herbs and brew remedies and preserve and prepare food.

Worshipped from the dawn of Egyptian history—the Goddess Isis—Goddess of Healing, the Divine Physician. Born in Egypt some 6000 years ago, she was an enlightened mortal raised to Goddess. Her dynasty of priestesses initiated women in the art of natural medicine, the mysteries of writing, agriculture, spinning, and weaving, and established the knowledge of humanism and the institute of matrimony.

The foremother of the Pagan faith, her teachings travelled the globe, emerging in every Goddess religion. The coveted bloodline of Isis, bestowed to the ruling families, brought wisdom and healing to the world and literally changed the face of the planet. It is believed that Isis was the first human born with a rounded forehead and two eyebrows instead of one—the unibrow. The matriarchs of the tribes, through selective breeding, cultivated her lineage for generations.

Many of the prayers in the Papyrus Ebers (one of the oldest preserved medical documents in the world) concerning women and childbirth are dedicated to Isis. She is shown holding the Ahnk, the symbol of Eternal Life

Isis taught her acolytes the magic arts and the mysteries of medicinal potions.

We are always amazed and mystified at the power of Nature as we sit outside every day watching our lovely garden come to life, pondering how it all starts from a tiny seed. Having, nurturing, and loving your garden throughout the seasons, being able to choose when to harvest—how to dry—what to prepare, makes a stronger offering . . .

Beans

"Sow peas and beans in the wane of the moon,
Who soweth them sooner, he soweth too soon,
That they with the planet may rest and rise,
And flourish with bearing, most plentiful-wise."[46]

"In the Garden
Shelling Peas
A little Magic for
Mary and Me"[47]

Nurture yourself. Live within the seasons and the cycles of the moon rather than in hours and even minutes. Reclaim your inner harmony; bring yourself down to Earth, appreciate nature and your fellow humans, bring about peace within your life and in the lives of the people around you.

Take the time to read, to write in a journal, to admire yourself, and take pride in your dress. Be happy, talk civilly. Heal yourself.

"Woodman, spare that tree!
    Touch not a single bough!
In youth it sheltered me,
    And I'll protect it now.
'Twas my forefather's hand
    That placed it near his cot;
There, woodman, let it stand,
    Thy axe shall harm it not.!

That old familiar tree,
    Whose glory and renoun
Are spread o'er the land and sea,
    And wouldst thou hew it down?
Woodman, forbear thy stroke!
    Cut not its earth-bound ties
O, spare that aged oak,
    Now towering to the skies!

When but an idle boy
    I sought its grateful shade;
In all there gushing joy
    Here, too, my sisters played.
My mother kissed me here;
    My father pressed my hand-
Forgive this foolish tear,
    But let that old oak stand!

My heart strings round thee cling,
    Close as thy bark, old friend!
Here shall the wild-bird sing,
    And still thy branches bend.
Old tree! The storm still brave!
    And, woodman, leave the spot;
While I've a hand to save,
    Thy axe shall harm it not."[48]

"The World is too much with us: late and soon,
       Getting and spending, we lay waste our powers:
       Little we see in nature that is ours;
We have given our hearts away, a sorted boon!

This sea that bares her bosom to the moon,
       The winds that will be howling at all hours
       And are up gathered now like sleeping flowers,
For this, for everything, we are out of tune;"[49]

"January Moon – ploughed soil
April Moon – germination moon, seed sowing
May Moon – planting moon, plants burst into life
December Moon – sap slow, time to prune trees
October Moon – harvest moon"[50]

Moon Planting

Plant above-ground crops (peas, beans, lettuce, cucumbers, tomatoes, herbs) when the moon is waxing and below-ground crop (root vegetables—potatoes, carrots, turnip, beets, onions) when the moon is waning. This will yield a healthier plant and a more ambrosial fruit.

Waxing and Waning

After the full moon, when the moon is getting smaller, is when the moon is *waning*. When there is no moon, (the *dark side of the moon*) and the moon is getting fuller, the moon is *waxing*.

Outdoor planting should be completed before the full moon in May as the moon pulls at the tides of the soil as well as the waters, causing the roots to reach out and embrace Mother Earth.

Rain Barrels. Waste not, want not. Any way of catching rainwater to water your garden is a good thing. To infuse life into your garden, pour in apple cider as you are turning the soil. Maximize your gardening space by growing herbs and food in pots indoors and outdoors.

Offerings in the way of food are the most natural way to ensure the magic will be received. Here are some ways to Give the Gifts of the Garden Goddess

Flowering herbs in the garden are a natural bee attractant, helping to pollinate the garden, ensuring a fruitful crop.

Harvesting Herbs and Flowers

To elicit the most potential, harvest in the early morning when the dew is still fresh on the plant. The first cuttings are the most auspicious for *Enchantments of the Heart*. Ask the plant for permission. Give it time to prepare itself and offer thanks for its life force

Drying: When it is time to harvest, clip the plants, leaving enough of the stem to tie a string around. Hang upside down in a cool, dry place. Put a clean white tea towel or piece of cardboard, not newspaper or printed paper, under the drying plants to catch any falling petals. Once the cuttings are sufficiently dried, clip the flowers and leaves off the stems and place in glass jars to keep the dust off and retain the potency, colour, and vibrancy of the plant.

The *Drying Basket*: We don't throw anything away. The excess clippings (including stems and throw-away leaves) we use in our smudging and spell work. Cloak your aura in the smoke of your offerings, but do not inhale directly.

Herbs you eat: Pinch the flower Herbs for magic—the blossom's the power.

Green Goddess Salad

Salad in a pot with a Well-Wishing for Fruition composed of edible flowers, herbs, and lettuces. Bestowing upon the recipient *Power of the Written Word* (see page #172), well-wishing Happiness, Prosperity, and Success with new opportunities.

Greens. Hand-in-hand with life, made ever more potent from the nurturing and energy of each element: Earth, Water, Air, and Fire (the life-giving Sun). Plant before the full moon and give your gift when the plants are young. As the plants grow, your wishing comes to fruition, and once eaten, benefits all who partake.

Happy Slug Death

Embed a dish in the dirt to the rim. Fill 2/3 full of beer. The slugs line up trying to get a drink. They slide in, get drunk, and drown a happy death.

Faerie Water

*"In the forest, the farmer's daughter
collecting blossoms for Faerie Water"*[51]

Faerie Water has been used since ancient times as a beauty treatment to refresh the skin and lure the boys with the romantic smell of flowers and spices on a Midsummer's Night. Enshrine the essence of the flowers and herbs from your garden or bouquet in an enchanted floral water that can be used in the bath, as a refreshing body splash or a cold mist spray on a hot summer day.

SUN TEA METHOD:

In the morning, pluck the small flowers off the herbs and the petals off the larger flowers. Clean in cool water (if there is any question of chemical spray, lightly wash them in any one of the organic vegetable-wash products on the market. Rinse well). Place in a jar that has a lid with a tight seal. Keep in mind, the more petals used, the stronger the concoction. Add distilled water: 2 cups water to 1 cup flowers. Put the lid on the jar and place it in the direct sunlight. Move throughout the day to catch the sun's full rays. At sunset strain the Sun Tea and pour the faerie water into a special coloured-glass bottle. Refrigerate and use within a week.

If you find yourself wanting to vamp together your own special brew on a rainy day, just add the herbs and flowers immediately to water that has just been boiled. Use the same proportions as the *Sun Tea* method. Steep for 10 minutes or so, strain, and bottle.

Sun Tea

Enchanted Bath Blessings

Bottled enticement—the ritual of bathing—to captivate and enthral your lover, to ground and purify, for protection and attraction.

The enchantment starts when you plant your garden. Choose a section for your sacred herbs, allowing them to flower for your spellwork. When mixing and conjuring bath salts, use the dry flowers and leaves you have collected for the blend. As you combine the coarse sea salt with the herbs, interweave your words, thus bestirring the magic as you speak and write your blessing.

BATH BLESSINGS

May you feel Loved and Beautiful
every time you Bathe.
As the Rosemary Salt dissolves may it
be a grounding force neutralizing
low spirits and heaviness of heart.
May the tang of the citrus tingle your spirit
as it refreshes your skin.

To exfoliate, rub the bath salts onto the skin and let fall into the bath. After the exfoliation, relax and receive the benefits of the salt and herbs.

ENCHANTED BATH BLENDS
to give to a friend, to entice a lover,
to heal a broken heart.

Herbs of Allure—Love Blends
~ Rosemary, lilac flowers, dried
   grapefruit, and lemon zest
~ Lavender with Mint and Basil flowers
~ Rose and pansy petals with Lemon
   Verbina leaves
~ Powdered milk with rose petals and
   Lavender

Ground and Purify
~ Salt and Parsley, a purifying bath
   to release negativity
~ Chamomile and Lavender to relax

Protection and Attraction
~ Sage – sacred and purifying
~ Mint and Lemon Verbina leaves
   for attraction
~ Celery leaf and Parsley flowers
   with dried Parsley seed

Love Tinctures & Elixirs

Through the spoken word women learned the country skill of simpling—the distillation of plants. They were taught the mysteries of plant lore and handed down favourite old family recipes containing time-honoured ingredients, seasoned with the essence of love and magic, harnessing the energy and the effect of each plant.

Potions, Tinctures, and Elixirs can give an offering of solace or jubilance, be restorative, enlightening, mystical, leaving you spellbound and enthralled, transported to a euphoric physical experience.

Raspberry Leaf and Raspberry:
Aphrodesiac – offers protection and love
Nutmeg, Poppyseed & Dried Pear:
Hypnotic seduction – love attractant
Lavender and Rose Petals:
Dream weaving–purification, happiness and relaxation
Chamomile Flowers and dried Cranberries:
Calming and balancing

Recipe: "Elixir Preparation" see page #177.

Dried herbs from the garden:
Oregano, Basil, and Thyme flowers

The Rose

"Tis said as Cupid danced among the
gods, he down the nectar flung,
Which, on the white rose being shed,
made it forever red."[52]

Rose, the Goddess Herb, steeped
in legend, has been used by our
foremothers in Folklore Cooking, Love
Potions, Charms, and Medicinal Remedies
for generations. The five-petal rose,
similar to the Alberta wild rose in Canada,
is the symbol of Womanhood. The five
petals represent the female cycle of life:
Infant, Child, Maid, Mother, and Crone.

The Rose has always been associated with love and lovemaking, brewed as an aphrodisiac, and used for spellwork
throughout the many journeys of past women's sexlore. One
of the most passionate romances in history, preserved by a
cherished legacy of letters, is the love affair of Josephine and
Napoleon Bonaparte.

Josephine, born in June 1763 (the month of the rose) on the
Caribbean island of St. Lucia, christened Marie Rose Tascher
de la Pagerie—was prophesied at birth to become queen.
Raised in Martinique by a Creole nanny, she was taught the
game of card divination and introduced to spirituality and
sortilege.

After the death of her husband and her imprisonment
during the "Terror" (the French Revolution), she became
bedmate to some of the most powerful and influential men
in post revolutionary France. Mesmerized by her captivating
sexuality, charm, and grace, Bonaparte proposes marriage.
She enchains him with a lust as no other woman had ever
done or ever would do (his dying word was "Josephine").
While on campaign, he would dream of the musky fragrance
of her sex; her floral scent would linger on her letters to drive
him mad with memories and desire.

Letter from Napoleon to Josephine:

"By what art is it that you have been able to captivate all my faculties, and to concentrate in yourself my moral existance? It is a magic, my sweet love, which will finish only with my life. To live for Josephine – there is the history of my life. I am trying to reach you – I am dying to be near you. Fool that I am I do not perceive that I increase the distance between us. What lands, what countries seperate us! What a time before you read these weak expressions of a troubled soul in which you reign! Ah! My adorable wife, I know what fate awaits me, but if it keep me much longer from you, it will be insupportable. I stop, my sweet love: my soul is sad – my body is fatigued – my head is giddy – men disgust me – I aught to hate them – they seperate me from my beloved."[53]

Josephine surrounded herself with beauty and feminism. Her intoxicating allure evolved from the seductive sound of her voice, like warm amber honey, and her perfume, the aphrodisiac scent of her famous rose garden in Malmaison.

Here are some ways you can manifest the "Language of Courtly Love" in your own relationship. Serve your loved one red wine with red rose petals sprinkled on top. Take your lover on a rose petal journey through the bathroom into the bedroom, from rose petals floating in a tub of water to petals strewn on the bed and pillows. Surround yourself with beautiful things; use the power of your femininity.

A Blessing of Love for family and friends can be as simple as serving a refreshing jug of water with a handful of fresh rose petals floating on top.

Invoke Your Lover

When you summon the mysticism of the rose, it brings harmony and balance, is calming, and at the same time, emotionally arousing, allowing you to let go of your daily conflicts. Smudging the petals opens communication to your lover, luring him back to you, calling upon him to reply.

A Break-Up Spell

Focusing intent on an object to manifest your objective goal is a powerful tool used by Wisewomen to change adverse circumstances.

Focus your intent on the rose you choose for this spell. Write the persons name on a plain piece of paper, and wrap it around the stem of the rose. Use twine to secure it. Envision the person in your mind's eye. As the flower dries up so does the love-affair.

Every time you look at the rose, keep this charm in your mind's eye.

"as the Bloom fades, so shall our love whither

as the Bloom fades, so shall our love whither"

Rose Strawberry Syrup

Rinse the flowers in cool water.
Pluck the petals off the flower.
Snip the white tip off each petal.
Wash 1 1/2 cups of strawberries.
Crush berries and place in a pot
Add:
1/2 cup prepared petals
1 cup of water,
2 tablespoons lemon juice
1/2 cup of sugar
Bring to a boil; reduce heat
Simmer for 5 minutes.
Let sit 10 minutes.
Pour through cheesecloth,
rendering a clear liquid.
Pour liquid back into the pot.
Add:
1 box vegetable pectin
1 cup water
Bring to a rolling boil.
Simmer for 15 minutes.
Add:
1 teaspoon of Rose Water
Pour into prepared jars
(see page #175).
Serve over French toast,
waffles, crepes, griddle cakes,
ice cream, desserts, or
your lover's body.

For the Vamp in all of us;
seduce and entice your
lover. After the dinner date,
invite your sweetheart for an
unforgettable dessert.

With this dish, you are Calling upon the *Power of Creation*. You are calling the Power and once it is there, you have to be a Willing Participant, allowing yourself to become entranced with desire and, with every bud and leaf, charged with passion. With each bud—like a woman's sexual flower, each petal like the petals of her opening—think of your innermost fantasies, sexual acts you would like to perform or, in turn, have done to you. As the bowl melts and each bud is released, know that each sexual act has reached its climax. Dreams can come true.

Recipe for the Rose Bowl
Take 2 bowls that are freezer safe (metal or plastic), one slightly smaller than the other. Pour 1/2 inch of water in the bottom of the larger bowl. Place small rose buds and a few leaves and petals in the water and freeze. (Make sure it is on a level surface.) Once the bottom layer is frozen, place the second bowl inside the first and add water almost to the rim. Place more small buds, petals, and leaves into the water around the bowls. Top up with water if you need to, and place into the freezer. Once the water is frozen, turn the bowls upside down and carefully run a trickle of hot water onto the larger bowl until you can remove it.

Now carefully run some hot water into the smaller bowl until *that* bowl can be removed, as well. (Do not add too much water to the inside of the bowl.) you may have to pour out the water (carefully) and repeat this process a few times before successfully removing the inner bowl. You have created your *Bowl of Allure* and ignited your inner desires—now you need to conjure the dessert and Summon Erotica into the atmosphere.

Conjuring the Dessert

Start marinating the fruit in the morning. Select fruit that will sit well in liqueur throughout the day. We like pears, cherries, strawberries, and firm raspberries. If you do not want alcohol, use plain honey (used in Indian Erotica Culture for generations). Strain the fruit just before serving and set aside the leftover liquid to add into the whipped cream (whip the cream first, then add the leftover honey or liqueur) or drizzle on top. Fresh rose petals give this Orgiastic *Lover's Dessert* the finishing touch.

Summoning Erotica

Put a container of the whipped cream in an ice bucket or big bowl of ice. Have a pot of honey heating over a votive candle. Gently heat the honey to your liking. Think of all the bodily places that can be lavished with whipped cream and honey (and, of course, licked off). Write them in a note and give it to your lover while you are enjoying your dessert. Make sure you include all the scenarios you have fantasized. Draw a rose-petal bath after the lovemaking.

You are conjuring the Magic of Sex.

Female Animal Magnetism

Each woman has her own personal sexual attractant, the enticing scent of her natural vaginal essence. Here we are offering a way for you to use your own innermost elixir to ignite desire.

This is best done when you are clean and healthy. When ovulating, you are at your most potent point. Start by having a shower. Pick an essential oil or perfume that speaks to you of romance and mixes well with your most intimate scent. Pour a small amount of the oil-perfume into a dish. Reach into your moist inner vagina and coat your fingers with the musky lubricant of your flower. Once vaginal fluid is on your fingers, dip them into the essential oil. Apply to your neck and wrists, in between your breasts, behind your ears. These are your pulse points; they heat up as your heart beats, getting hotter as your heart beats faster, releasing your own musky attractant that is exotic and irresistible.

HOW TO

"We are the music
makers,
And we are the
dreamers of dreams,
Wandering by lone
sea-breakers,
And sitting by
desolate streams;
World-losers and
world-forsakers,
On whom the pale
moon gleams:
Yet we are the movers
and shakers
Of the world for ever,
it seems."[54]

The Power of the Spoken Word

To use the *Power of the Spoken Word,* vocally project vibrations to the Universe by chanting and using poetic blessings to actualize the force of attraction. Some of the most successful askings have been written by hand and conjured by a single person.

Incantations have both rhyme and reason; they enforce what is wanted by use of repetition, weaving the beauty of words into the vibrations of magic. Your personal invocation can be more powerful when you create your own poem or blessing.

Visualize internal light and create a vibration, chanting and repeating your incantation to yourself or back and forth between two people, creating the potency of the words to manifest an answer and bring about satisfaction.

The Power of the Written Word

The *Power of the Written Word*: Here we are using the hand-written word as an offering and delivering it to the Universe by way of smoke and fire.

On a plain piece of paper, pen your request with grace and thankfulness, signing it with your full name. Place your asking in a fireproof smudge pot along with some herbs or spices as an offering (dry the clippings from your garden that you don't use for simples or cooking). Using a candle, light the paper on fire and allow the smoke to bring about a universal reaction; sulphur from a match can shift the result.

Songwriting and Poetry have been used for blessings, askings, and giving thanks by Healers and Wisewomen for generations. Write your own or use a poem that is relevant to the situation.

How To

How to make stew gravy:
Take a plastic bag, put 1 to 2 cups of flour into it (depending on how much meat you are using), add some spices—Rosemary, Basil, Oregano, salt and pepper. Shake well; place stew meat into the bag a handful at a time. Shake well again, making sure to coat each piece of meat on all sides with a generous dusting of the flour/herb mixture.

Pour enough oil into your stew pot to generously cover the bottom about 1/4 inch deep. Grapeseed oil is wonderful; it can be heated to a high temperature without burning. Heat the oil so that the meat sizzles when dropped in. Take the meat out of the bag and lightly shake off the excess flour; place into the pot of hot oil. Sprinkle a small bit of the spiced flour on top of the meat. Add some finely cut onions and garlic—celery leaf adds a great taste—and brown the meat on every side to the point of almost burning it.

Add water to cover the meat and simmer for a few minutes, stirring with a wooden spoon and scraping the bottom of the pot to mix in the flour that has stuck to it. Add more water to make enough gravy for your stew; let the meat simmer for at least 1 1/2 to 2 hours to allow the meat to tenderize.

At this point, add your vegetables, then your spices at the end (add spices 20 minutes or so before your dish is done because spices are at their best when not overcooked).

How to thicken gravy without lumps: Take one small jar; add 3 heaping tablespoons of flour and 1 teaspoon of white granulated sugar (the sugar mixes with the flour causing no lumps to occur). Put on the lid and shake vigorously. Now add 1 1/2 cups of water and shake again. Slowly add this to your drippings.

How to darken chicken gravy: Add 2 to 3 sun-dried tomatoes to the bottom of the pan. Use the water from your boiled potatoes or carrots.

How to sterilize a jar: Take a flat pan, add cold water (1 1/2 inch), place a clean jar upside down into the water. If you are using an old jar with a glass lid, put the lid into the water also. Bring the water to a boil, and immediately turn the temperature down until the water begins to simmer. Leave for 4 to 5 minutes.

How to seal a jar or bottle lid with wax: In a small pot on medium heat, melt 1 block of paraffin wax. Put the lid on your bottle (be sure it is on tight enough not to leak into the wax). Now turn your bottle upside down and dip the top of the bottle into the wax, then quickly remove it. Do not heat the wax too hot or it gets too thin and will not adhere to the bottle. Store at a temperature that will not melt the wax.

How to grate tomatoes: This is easier than the peeling process. Simpley slice the tomato in half and using a grater, grate until only the skin is left.

How to dry fresh ginger for cooking and brewing: Cut the Ginger into thin slices and place on a flat rock or ceramic tile on a stove burner (lowest setting) or on the warmer element. Dry thoroughly by turning every hour.

How to dry pears and apples: The best way to dry fruit is by placing thin slices on a flat screen in the direct sun for 3 to 4 days. When that is not possible, preheat the oven to 200 degrees, place the clean, sliced fruit on a baking sheet lined with 2 layers of parchment paper. Bake at 200 degrees for 5 to 6 hours.

How to make home-style pancakes with a mix: Add yogurt, hot water, and milk in equal parts, to make up the cup of milk required.

How to sour milk: Add 1 tablespoon of white vinegar to 1 cup of milk.

How to tell when the cake is baked: Insert a toothpick into the middle of the cake. If it comes out clean, the cake is done.

How to make the best rice pudding: Use Arborio rice. The grain stays firm.

How to cook without the meat sticking to the grill on an openfire or barbeque: Pour 1/2 inch of olive oil into a bowl. Cut a medium onion in half, stick a fork into it and dip the cut end into the bowl of oil. Rub the onion onto the grill before you place the meat on it. Repeat if necessary.

How to create your own _Still Room_: Choose a meditative workplace in a cool dark area or room. Use that space for drying and storing herbs and preparing folkloric remedies, recipes, and crafts.

Bowl of Tricks: In a large bowl use your dry onion and garlic skins to absorb the moisture from the hot peppers after the summer harvest.

Love Tinctures & Elixirs

Prepare your dried fruit and herbal concoction. Take a sterilized jar and place the mixture loosely into the jar, arranging the herbs in a comely fashion. Fill your jar 3/4 full with your choice of spirits (we prefer Vodka); add 1/4 cup sugar for each cup of alcohol (if you find it too sweet, use less sugar). The sugar increases the strength of the brew. Top up the bottle with the rest of the alcohol, tightly screw on the lid, or seal the lid with wax. Set in a cool, dark place for 2 to 3 weeks.

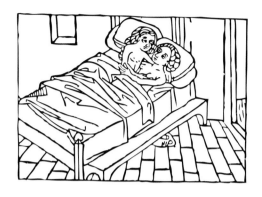

Decoction: Extracts the active ingredient. To prepare a decoction, simmer the herb's root or bark in water for 5 to 20 minutes, depending on the plant.
Infusion: Add boiling water to medicinal herbal leaves and flowers and steep in a tea-like fashion.
Tincture: An elixir made by distilling a herb or fruit in alcohol (use only organic produce).

acknowledgements

We would like to offer our heartfelt thanks to . . .

Ramin Sabour and Casimir Loeber – Base-10 Design & Development Inc.
Jenn and Steve Bebb – Bebb Studios
April Peters – House Gallery Boutique
Robert Mackwood – Seventh Avenue Literary Agency
Maria T. Holman
Candyce Raymond
Laurie Greenwood
Val Wilson
Jorge Rocha – Friesens
Valley Hennell
Hoi Yu
Shawn Hossein and Meg Sistani – Universal Printing
Caitríona uí Mhuircheartaigh
The Librarians at:
University College Dublin
Lambeth Palace Library,
Simon Fraser University
Liwayway Merlin
Jina Ryan
Nicole Hobbs
Heath Beggs
Jon Gabriel
Julian Ayers
Jana Lynn White
Mr. and Mrs. Pickwell
Sam and Bob Nason
Dave – Dave's Farm Market
Sheida Tabeshfar
Echos Discontinued China & Silver

Mary Edwards and Shannon Loeber
live in North Vancouver, British Columbia,
on Canada's spectacular West Coast.

For more information, please visit our blog
at www.wisewomanscookery.com.

Bibliography

Permissions Granted

Page 22
Collier, John. Britain, 1850 – 1934. **Priestess of Delphi**. 1891, London. oil on canvas. 160.0 x 80.0 cm. Gift of the Rt. Honourable, the Earl of Kintore 1893. Art Gallery of South Australia, Adelaide.

Lefebvre, Jules Joseph. **Clemence Isaure**. Image thanks to the Art Renewal Center®. www.artrenemal.org.

Page 30
Song by Patrick Daley. National Folklore Collection. University College Dublin. NFC 782, 54 - 55.

Page 34
Hunt, William Holman. **Isabella and the pot of Basil**. Laing Art Gallery. Tyne & Wear archives and museums.

Page 44
la Papesse, with the authorization of FRANCE CARTES GRIMAUD.

Page 54
Waterhouse, John William, 1849. **Tristan and Isolde**. Image thanks to the Art Renewal Center®. www.artrenemal.org.

Page 72
XIR34891. Credit: **Still Life**. 1640 (oil on canvas) by Jan Davidsz. de Heem (1606-84). Louvre, Paris, France// The Bridgeman Art Library. Nationality / copyright status: Dutch / out of copyright.

Page 82
Sandys, Frederick. **Morgan-Le-Fay**. ©Birmingham Museums & Art Gallery.

Page 91
Baker, Margaret. **Gardener's Magic and Folklore**. Used with permission from Rizzoli International Publications, Inc.

Page 96
Follower of Jacopo Tintoretto. **Portrait of Veronica Franco**. Worcester Art Museum. Worcester, Massachusetts. Austin S. Garver Fund and Sarah C. Garver Fund.

Poems and Selected Letters / Veronica Franco. Edited and translated by Ann Rosalind Jones and Margaret F. Rosenthal. p. cm. — (The other voice in early modern Europe). The University of Chicago Press. Chicago 60637. The University of Chicago Press, Ltd. London. © 1998 by the University of Chicago. All rights reserved. Published 1998.

Page 102
Gervex, Henri. (1852-1929). **Rolla.** 1878. Oil on canvas. 173 x 200 cm. Location: Musee des Beaux-Arts. Bordeaux, France. Photo Credit: Erich Lessing / Art Resource, NY.

Page 108
Bouguereau, William-Adolphe (1825-1905). **Flora and Zephyr**. Canvas. Location: Musee des Beaux-Arts. Bordeaux, France. Photo Credit: Erich Lessing / Art Resource, NY. Image Reference: ART172475.

Page 109
Wolkstein, Diane and Kramer, Samuel Noah. *Inanna, Queen of Heaven and Earth: Her Stories and Hymns from Sumer.* © Diane Wolkstein.

Illustration. © Stéphane. Beaulieu, after Gadon 1989:137. "Uruk Vase, with procession of naked priests carrying gifts to Inanna's shrine., Inanna greeting them at its door marked by her gateposts. Alabaster. 3'. Uruk, Mesopotamia. Fourth millennium BCE." © J. Stuckey. Matrifocus. Imbolc 2005 Vol 4 - 2 – Inanna and the "Sacred Marriage."

Illustration. © Stéphane Beaulieu, after Meador 2000: 59. "Dumuzi (man in net kilt; see Steinkeller 1999: 104-111) approaching Inanna at shrine, procession of naked priests following, with gifts. Reconstruction. Alabaster Vase. 3'. Fourth millennium BCE. Uruk, Mesopotamia." © J. Stuckey. Matrifocus. Imbolc 2005 Vol 4 - 2 – Inanna and the "Sacred Marriage."

Illustration. © Stéphane Beaulieu, after Teubal 1983: 117. "Couple on terracotta bed, perhaps representing the "Sacred Marriage." Object could have been bought at the festival. Mesopotamia 3rd. millennium BCE." © J. Stuckey. Matrifocus. Imbolc 2005 Vol 4 - 2 – Inanna and the "Sacred marriage."

© Stuckey, Professor Johanna. Quote from **Sacred Prostitutes**. MatriFocus. Cross-Quarterly for the Goddess Woman. Samhain 2005 Vol 5-1

Page 110
18th and 19th century erotic books owned by author and art collector Roger Peyrefitte were auctioned off and dispersed in 1981. Frontispice and engravings from "L'Aretin by Agostino Carracci, or eroti. Location: Private Collection. Photo Credit: Erich Lessing / Art Resource, NY. Image Reference : ART171435

Barnstone, Tony and Ping, Chou. **Fruit Plummets from the Plum Tree**, from *The Anchor Book of Chinese Poetry*. Copyright ©2005 by Tony Barnstone and Chou Ping. Used by permission of Anchor Books, a division of Random House, Inc.

Page 112
Sodoma, Giovanni Antonio Bazzi, called II (1477-1549). Alexander the Great and Roxanne. Detail from the **Wedding of Alexander the Great and Roxanne**. Fresco. Location: Villa Farnesina, Rome, Italy. Photo Credit: Scala / Art Resource, NY. Image Reference: ART128693.

Page 114
Yanagawa, Shigenobu. Japan, 1787 – 1832. **Two lovers**. c. 1800-25, Japan. nishiki-e, oban, colour woodblock print. 25.0 x 37.0 cm. South Australian Government Grant 2005. Art Gallery of South Australia, Adelaide.

Page 115
Courtesans of Daimonjiya Viewing Cherry Blossoms. From the collection of Scripps College, Claremont, CA.

Page #119
Stone relief sculpture of the goddess Brigantia depicting the native goddess of North Britain in the guise of Minerva, from Birrens. SCOTLANDSIMAGES.COM National Museums of Scotland CAA00133.

Duncan, John. **Saint Bride**. Tempera on canvas. THE NATIONAL GALLERY OF SCOTLAND.

A Companion Guide to the National Gallery of Scotland, Edinburgh, National Galleries of Scotland, 2002.

Page 122
Compliments of E. de Grandmont Inc.

Page123
Fouquet, Jean. **Madonna**. KMSKA, copyright Lukas-Art in Flanders vzw. Photo Hugo Maertens.

Page 130
Gillray, James. **Ci-devant occupations - or - Madame Talian and the Empress Josephine dancing**. ©National Portrait Gallery. London.

Page 131
Isabey, Jean-Baptiste (1767-1855). Portrait of Theresa de Cabarrus (1773-1835) also known as **Madame Tallien**. Bibliothèque nationale de France.

Page 135
Illustration **Morgan Le Fay Casts Away The Scabbard** reproduced with permission from the publisher of *King Arthur - Tales from the Round Table*, Andrew Lang, Editor, H. J. Ford, Illustrator, Copyright 2002, Dover Publications, Inc.

Page 136
Leighton, Frederic (1830-1896). **Garden of the Hesperides**. Ca. 1892. Oil on canvas. Location: Lady Lever Art Gallery. Port Sunlight, Great Britain. Photo Credit: Visual Arts Library / Art Resource, NY. Image Reference: ART371438.

Page 137
Burne-Jones, Edward (1833-1898) and John Henry Dearle (1860-1932). **Pomona**. c. 1900. Tapestry-woven wool and silk on a cotton warp. 168.9 x 109.2 cm. Made by Morris & Company. Inv.: T.33-1981. Location: Victoria and Albert Museum. London, Great Britain. Photo Credit: Victoria & Albert Museum, London / Art Resource, NY. Image Reference: ART116709.

Usage rights for Pepin Press images (book, article of "Wassail", and apple cider drink from England). "images taken from book *Graphic Frames* from The Pepin Press (or www.pepinpress.com)

Page 160
WDM27975. Credit: **The Love Potion**. 1903 (oil on canvas) by Evelyn De Morgan (1855-1919). © The De Morgan Centre. London. The Bridgeman Art Library. Nationality / copyright status: English / out of copyright.

Page 162
Viger du Vigneau, Jean Louis (1819-1879). **The Rose of Malmaison**. **Salon of 1866**. Oil on canvas. 71 x 92 cm. Photo: Arnaudet. Location: Chateaux de Malmaison et Bois-Preau, Rueil-Malmaison, France. Photo Credit: Réunion des Musées Nationaux / Art Resource, NY. Image Reference: ART168523.

Chapter Bibliography by Page

Cover
Colour Portrait by Bebb Studios. www.bebbstudios.com

HERBAL LORE

Page 4
1. James Mew and John Ashton. *Drinks of The World*. New York: Charles Scribner's & Sons, 1892 (University College Dublin: UCD)

Page 5
2, 3. C. L'Estrange Ewen. *Witchcraft and Demonianism*. London: Heath Cranton Ltd., 1933 (UCD)

Page 12
4, 5. Sir William Turner Thistleton-Dyer. *The Folklore of Plants*. London: Chatto & Windus, Piccadilly, 1889 (UCD) Hand Drawing of Rosemary by Shannon Loeber.

Page 15
6. Shannon Loeber and Mary Edwards
7. Louis Untermeyer. *This Singing World*. Harcourt Brace & Company, 1923. (Book of Knowledge – Vol. 2, pg 737)

Page 18
8. C. V. Loeber

Page 19
Colour Portrait by Bebb Studios. www.bebbstudios.com

Page 23
Photograph of Bay Leaf by Ramin Sabour

Page 26
Faerie Border Illustration by Candyce Raymond

Page 29
9. Patrick Daley. (Song). Ireland: Department of Folklore. (UCD)

Page 33
Hand Drawing of Basil by Shannon Loeber

Page 34
10. John Keats. 1884. Isabella; or, The Pot of Basil. *A Story from Boccaccio.*

Page 36
11. Dictionary.com
12. Sir William Turner Thistleton-Dyer. *The Folklore of Plants.* London: Chatto & Windus, Piccadilly, 1889 (UCD)

SPICE SORCERY

Page 42
13. Geoffrey Chaucer. *The Canterbury Tales.*

Page 43
Colour Portrait by Bebb Studios. www.bebbstudios.com
14. The Hymn of Renenutet. Wikipedia.org - the free encyclopedia created and edited by online user community.

Page 47
15. John Gay. 1685 – 1732. **The Spell**. Porteaus, Alexander. *Forest Folklore, Mythology and Romance.* London: George Allen & Unwin Ltd., 1928 (UCD)

Page 50
Colour Portrait by Bebb Studios. www.bebbstudios.com

Page 56
16. Art of the Heart Invocation by Shannon Loeber and Mary Edwards

Page 58
Corsette by April Peters – House Gallery Boutique. 2865 West 4th, Vancouver BC. www.velvetandlace.com

Page 60
17. Samuel Lover. 1797- 1868. **When the Sun Sinks to Rest**. *Songs and Ballads by Samuel Lover.* Fourth Edition. London: Houlston and Wright. 1858.

Page 67
Colour Portrait by Bebb Studios. www.bebbstudios.com

Page 68
18. "The Technique". Anonymous Quote.

BOUNTIFUL EARTH FRUITS & VEGETABLES

Page 70
19. Joshua Sylvester. 1563 – 1618. **Were I as Base As Is The Lowly Plain**. The Grolier Society Ltd. *The Book of Knowledge.* Toronto: Educational Book Company Ltd., 1949

Page 73
20. Thomas Bailey Aldrich. 1836 – 1908. Stedman, Edmund Clarence. *An American Anthology.* 1787 – 1900.

Page 79
Hand Drawing of Tomato by Shannon Loeber

Page 83
Colour Portrait by Bebb Studios. www.bebbstudios.com

Page 88
21. Thomas Moore. 1779-1852. **The Potato**.

Page 91
22. Margaret Baker. *Gardener's Magic and Folklore.* Used with permission from Rizzoli International Publications, Inc.

Page 92
23. John Parkinson. 1567 - 1650. *Paradise in Sole* (1629)

Page 96
24, 25. *Poems and selected letters / Veronica Franco.* Edited and translated by Ann Rosalind Jones and Margaret F. Rosenthal. p. cm. — (The other voice in early modern Europe). The University of Chicago Press. Chicago 60637. The University of Chicago Press, Ltd. London. © 1998 by the University of Chicago. All rights reserved. Published 1998.

Page 97
Colour Portrait by Bebb Studios. www.bebbstudios.com

Page 100
26, 27, 28. Science Daily. February 16, 2007. www.sciencedaily.com

Page 102
Demitasse cups compliments of Echo's Discontinued China & Silver. www.echoschina.com

Page 108
29. One of Chichester Graces. Written in Goodwood Gardens, September, 1750. *The Works of the English Poets*, from Chaucer to Cowper: 1810. (SFU)
30. From: Kyriazis, Constantine D. *Eternal Greece.* Translated by Harry T. Hionides

Page 109
31. © Professor Johanna Stuckey. Quote from **Sacred Prostitutes**. *MatriFocus. Cross-Quarterly for the Goddess Woman.* Samhain 2005 Vol 5-1
32, 33, 34. © Diane Wolkstein. Diane Wolkstein and Samuel Noah Kramer. *Inanna, Queen of Heaven and Earth: Her Stories and Hymns from Sumer.* © Diane Wolkstein.

Page 111
35. Tony Barnstone and Chou Ping. **Fruit Plummets from the Plum Tree**. *The Anchor Book of Chinese Poetry*. Copyright ©2005 by Tony Barnstone and Chou Ping. Used by permission of Anchor Books, a division of Random House, Inc.

Page 114
36. Sanpu (1647-1732)

Page 119
37. Francine Nicholson. **What Do We Really Know?** *Celtic Well E-Journal* © 1999. Electronic version. http://www.applewarrior.com/celticwell/ejournal/imbolc/brighid.htm
38. A Companion Guide to the National Gallery of Scotland, Edinburgh, National Galleries of Scotland, 2002

Page 122
39. Robert Herrick. 1591-1674.

Page 123
40. **The Works of Voltaire: A Contemporary Version**. [The Maid of Orleans, V. I]. Volume: 40. Contributors: Tobias Smollett, unknown, William F. Fleming - translator, Voltaire - author, John Morley - unknown. Publisher: E. R. DuMont. Place of Publication: Paris. Publication Year: 1901. In reference to Agnes Sorel.

Page 125
Colour Portrait by Bebb Studios. www.bebbstudios.com

Page 129
Colour Portrait by Bebb Studios. www.bebbstudios.com
41. Browning, Robert (1812-1889). **In a Gondola**.

Page 132
42. *Plant-Lore & Garden-Craft of Shakespeare*. 1884. Poem by Thomas Tusser. 1524 -1580.

Page 136
43. John Milton. 1608-1674.

GARDEN ALCHEMY

Page 144
44. Sir William Turner Thistleton-Dyer. *The Folklore of Plants*. London: Chatto & Windus, 1889. (UCD)

Page 145
45. **Garden Goddess** by Shannon Loeber

Page 148
46. Sir William Turner Thistleton-Dyer. *The Folklore of Plants*. London: Chatto& Windus, Piccadilly, 1889 (UCD)
47. Poem by Shannon Loeber

Page 149
48. George Pope Morris. 1802-1864. **Woodman, Spare That Tree**. The Grolier Society Ltd. *The Book of Knowledge*. Volume 7. 1949.

Page 151
49. William Wordsworth. 1770-1850. **The World Is Too Much With Us; Late And Soon**.

Page 152
50. Margaret Baker.

Page 156
51. Poem by Shannon Loeber

Page 161
52. Robert Herrick. 1591-1674. Sir William Turner Thistleton-Dyer. *The Folklore of Plants*. London: Chatto& Windus, Piccadilly, 1889 (UCD)

Page 162
53. *The Court and Camp of Bonaparte*. Harper & Brothers. New York. 1842.

HOW TO

Page 170
54. Arthur O'Shaughnessy. 1884-1889. **The Dreamers of Dreams**. The Grolier Society Ltd. *The Book of Knowledge*. Volume 9. 1949.

Conversion Table

Volume Conversions

Customary quantity	Metric equivalent
1 teaspoon	5 mL
1 tablespoon or 1/2 fluid ounce	15 mL
1 fluid ounce or 1/8 cup	30 mL
1/4 cup or 2 fluid ounces	60 mL
1/3 cup	80 mL
1/2 cup or 4 fluid ounces	120 mL
2/3 cup	160 mL
3/4 cup or 6 fluid ounces	180 mL
1 cup or 8 fluid ounces or half a pint	240 mL
1 1/2 cups or 12 fluid ounces	350 mL
2 cups or 1 pint or 16 fluid ounces	475 mL
3 cups or 1 1/2 pints	700 mL
4 cups or 2 pints or 1 quart	950 mL
4 quarts or 1 gallon	3.8 L

Weight Conversions

Customary quantity	Metric equivalent
1 ounce	28 g
4 ounces or 1/4 pound	113 g
1/3 pound	150 g
8 ounces or 1/2 pound	230 g
2/3 pound	300 g
12 ounces or 3/4 pound	340 g
1 pound or 16 ounces	450 g
2 pounds	900 g

INDEX